How Story
Sparks Diversity,
Inclusion, and
Engagement

Sylvia Lafair

CEO
PUBLISHING

Disclaimers

No patent liability is assumed with respect to the use of the information contained herein.

Although every precaution has been taken in the preparation of this book, the publisher and author assume no responsibility for errors or omissions.

Neither is any liability assumed for damages resulting from the use of the information contained herein.

While all the stories are true, the names and companies have been changed to protect the privacy of the individuals.

Copyright © 2014 Sylvia Lafair, PhD

ISBN 978-0-9883625-1-2

Printed in the United States of America
Published April 2014

45 Country Place Lane
White Haven, PA 18661
Phone: 570-636-3858
Fax: 570-636-5387
sylvia@ceoptions.com
www.ceoptions.com

Praise for Unique

"It is amazing to have people be able to tell their stories and answer the question 'Who am I?' with more than 'I am a journalist' or 'I am the CEO.' SANKOFA Mapping™ is a powerful tool for all professionals to enhance their careers."
  – *Tyler Mathisen; co-anchor of CNBC's Power Lunch and Nightly Business on Public Television*

"Sylvia's work can help everyone at work benefit from seeing all the 'stuff' that goes on day after day that inhibits great outcomes and what to do about it. Learning how family patterns show up at work is extremely important for positive team engagement."
  – *Matthew Emmens; past CEO of Shire Pharmaceuticals and retired Chairman, CEO, and President of Vertex Pharmaceuticals*

"I have learned so much that is useful in my family business by doing my SANKOFA Map™ and looking at the patterns that are there from generation to generation. Finding the right stories to tell our employees about the business started by my grandfather, continued by my father, and now by my siblings and me is invaluable."
  – *Scott Williams; President, Williams Tire Company*

"I work directly with employees and their problems every day. Dr. Lafair's methods have a profound impact on my ability to help those who come to me rethink issues around conflict and quickly make positive changes. The methods in this book are UNIQUE."
  – *Brenda Thompson; Director of Human Resources at Morris, Nichols, Arsht & Tunnell LLP*

"Storytelling and relationships are at the heart of Dr. Lafair's magic touch. Readers find useful how-to questions to pull out pieces of their own stories that will take them to the next levels of personal development and leadership."
  – *Ann Booth-Barbarin; Senior Counsel and Assistant Secretary, Astra-Zeneca Pharmaceuticals*

UNIQUE: How Story Sparks Diversity, Inclusion, and Engagement

"Throughout your life you will hear people refer to 'connecting the dots' as the key to many things. I'm here to tell you that connecting the dots is the easy part. FINDING the dots is where the hard work lies. Dr. Lafair's SANKOFA™ method provided me with new, powerful tools for both personal discovery and helping me talk with my team at work in more effective ways."
  – Frank Walsh; Gen'l. Mgr. of Engineering, F.L. Smidth Co.

"SANKOFA Mapping™ is life-changing. Not only do I see my life in new and creative ways, it has helped me listen to others with more compassion and understanding. We do not have to tell our whole story at work; however, in knowing what happened through my lineage I am more self-aware and this has made me a better leader."
  – Yvonne Cangalosi; President, SPEX Certiprep

"An insightful book which gives a reflective voice to the experiences that shaped how we interact at work. A must-read for all who live with diversity and inclusion."
  – Kenneth L. Johnson; President, East Coast Executives

"Sylvia Lafair's books bring a rare view of 'systems' and 'systems thinking' that is helpful to individuals and families as well as business people working to build appreciation, cohesion, and success."
  – Frances Hesselbein; Chairman and founding President of Leader to Leader Institute

"Dr. Lafair graciously agreed to do coaching with me when I started my painting business in Houston, Texas. This job was a far cry from my youth when I was into drugs, crime, and eventually prison. I read her books and studied all I could about how the past impacts the present. Doing my SANKOFA Map™ was life-changing; so life-changing that I now have a PhD in Christian counseling. She is my major mentor."
  – Delmar Tillis; Jail Chaplain, Department of Justice, San Francisco, California

Sylvia Lafair, PhD

Dedication

I dedicate this book to my mother, Reba Colton Lafair, who was the rebel in her family of ten children and always was saying "there has to be a better way." As she grew to adulthood she became a community organizer before the term was formalized, a passion even into her late 70's when she started the first senior program in her neighborhood for elders to share their stories.

I also dedicate this book to everyone who has said, "It will stop with me" to speak out against discrimination; and to everyone who has ever said, "It will start with me," and created programs about innovative ways to bring people together.

UNIQUE: How Story Sparks Diversity,
Inclusion, and Engagement

Sylvia Lafair, PhD

Acknowledgments

This book sits at the core of who I am and is a culmination of so many years of searching for ways to get beyond constant conflict to develop creative and cooperative work environments. The rich dialogues I have had with colleagues and clients were the pulse beat of "and what else is there, and how else can we do it."

To the hundreds of you who have gone through Total Leadership Connections™ and stood at that flip chart filled with circles and squares admitting to that uncomfortable feeling in the pit of your stomach, and telling your story regardless, I salute you.

Special appreciation to those in leadership positions who saw the benefit of participating in this "before its time" Total Leadership Connections™ program, and offered the opportunity to others in their organizations. And to those who brought whole teams together to learn to be aware of their patterns through the OUT Technique™ and PEP Talks™.

Those who have stood with me as this method developed from "odd" to "unique." From "You've got to be kidding; we are going to talk about family patterns!" until it transformed into "Oh, now I get the family-work connections."

For all your support, thank you Ann Booth-Barbarin, Astra-Zeneca; Debra Neill, Neill Corporation; Edwin Neill, Neill Corporation; Brian Keefe, Bridge Gap Engineering; Frank Walsh, F.L. Smidth Co; Carole Haas Gravanio, Chair of Play on Philly; Andrew Cornell, Cornell Iron Works; Lauretta O'Hara, Cornell Iron Works; Linda Brewer, past Superintendent of Derry Township; Jackie Castleman, Principle at Derry Township; Bill, Scott and Jason Williams, Williams Tire

Company; Nancy Singer, Merck Pharmaceuticals; Lynn Rolston retired from California Pharmaceutical Association; Lucinda Maine, American Association of College Pharmacists; Michael MacDowell, retired President of Misericordia University; James Judd M.D., Horsham Physicians Group; Debbie Miller, Horsham Physicians Group; Nancy Pennebaker, Capay Valley Vision; Cynthia Tom, A Place of Her Own; Marylynn Sauro, Novartis; Joanne LaMarca NBC Universal; Tyler Mathisen, CNBC; Brenda Thompson, head of HR at Morris, Nichols, Arsht and Tunnell.

To my "power three" Debbie Woldanski, Fran Heithaus, and Tracy Wren for keeping the office running smoothly and keeping track of me wherever I am on this big planet, special hugs.

My family continues to be that supportive bedrock for all kinds of creative discussions that make us all that much better. Mikayla, Julie, Mark, Arielle and Dylan, keep questioning and searching; and to Herb, my partner in life's adventure, let's just keep going and growing.

Table of Contents

Introduction

"Somewhere between right and wrong there is a field; I'll meet you there" –Rumi

Can you remember the first time words were thrown your way that would bite and sting? Was it the color of your skin, the shape of your eyes? Perhaps you had a "funny" accent that someone imitated and you stopped talking. Did you live on the "other" side of town or wear out-of-style, hand-me-down clothes? Did you go to the "wrong" church? Were you too fat, thin, tall, short? Can you remember?

Anita, a well-respected corporate lawyer, participated in a leadership and diversity program based on the power of story and she responded to the question, "Can you remember?"

> *She was just turning four, playing with her next-door neighbor in the yard. She ran in the house to tell her mother she needed a bath. It was the middle of the afternoon and her mother said, "Honey, you were just playing outside for ten minutes; you are clean and fine."*
>
> *"No," Anita insisted. "Mary told me to go home and wash the dirt from my body, and I NEED a bath right now."*
>
> *Her mother took a deep breath and explained to her little girl that she was NOT dirty; it was just that her skin was naturally that beautiful cocoa color.*
>
> *The little girl marched out to announce this was her real skin color, only to come back crying, "Mary said she would not play with me until my skin was clean and white."*

Anita looked at her business colleagues and sighed. "You know that rhyme 'sticks and stones can break your bones but words can never hurt you?' Of course it is not true! One word or a snide smile can bring back all the slings and arrows and hurts of yesterday."

"What do you do," she asked her colleagues, leaders in a variety of business settings, "when someone at work says something unfair or unkind to you? Do you shut down and walk away; retort and play the gotcha game; complain to Human Resources?

"I am so tired of all the legal work I have to do around the still-unsettled area of diversity. I am yearning for change and yet...." her voice trailed off.

This diversity book is in response to "and yet...."

This book is about the words, actions, sticks, and stones that still abound in the workplace and leave us hurt and disappointed; and what to do about it.

It is about the power of our stories to make real and lasting change at work. It is about the way OUT, to Observe, Understand, and Transform ingrained yet out-dated beliefs and behavior patterns that no longer serve in this multicultural, global world.

While diversity programs that give a broad overview of gender, race, and cultural differences have been a starting point, they have not led to long-term change. More is needed.

It is time for diversity management to reinvent itself.

We need a road map that includes a mindset change for both individual input and team collaboration. We need to go upriver to find the multiple sources of the toxins that cause class action and hostile work environment lawsuits.

This is my story in response to "Can you remember?"

> *When I was in second grade, a group of us from the local elementary school would walk home with a sixth grader. I loved the freedom and the fun. We always took the same route. ... And then there was THAT day.*
>
> *THAT day was when a group of "big kids" from the Catholic School we passed every day started to throw stones at us and call us "Jesus killers" and "dirty Jews."*

THAT day and those words still ring in my grown-up head and make me both mad and sad. And now, well into the 21st Century, we continue to live in a world of judging, blaming, and attacking.

Have there been changes? Sure. We put a biracial man into the presidency of the United States. A Caucasian mayor elected in New York is married to an African-American woman and minimal comments abound.

However, the media thrives on controversy and loves to paint differences in big, bold sentences: who can be rated as better, worse, fat, thin, smart, dumb, sexy, or stupid. Being different gets the headlines.

People are either shunned or applauded for being strange, weird, and different; most importantly, they get noticed.

"Be different at whatever cost" is the media mantra.

EXCEPT in the workplace! In the workplace the game continues to be safety and conformity. Political correctness is still the norm. If you want to say something, say it softly, whisper, gossip, or just look away.

It is the silent infection. There is fear of retribution and only occasionally is there someone willing to stand up and speak out.

What is discussed here is a new kind of diversity management that is embedded right into professional development. It is not an extra "check the box" program. It is about the power of story, yours and mine, and how our stories, used effectively, can create organizational environments of trust, creativity, and productivity.

Knowing when and how to interject your story at work results in a deep level of cultural competence, career advancement, and inclusive team management.

As Harvard professor Howard Gardner states, "Stories are the single most-powerful weapon in a leader's arsenal."

This book will address a lasting type of leadership development that helps you access the deepest level of your authentic self in both thought and action. It means bringing your whole self to work; where you can be real and open without game-playing and pretense.

Once authenticity is unleashed there is no longer the need to participate at work with only one hand while the other is holding up a shield for protection.

My shield went up early, when the name-calling started.

"Jesus killer?" At age seven I really had very little idea about Jesus.

My elementary school was filled with kids who celebrated Christmas, while we did Chanukah. Not much was ever talked about in terms of religion. We were too young and more interested in playing tag and learning arithmetic. It was a peaceful coexistence of live and let live; at least for the little kids.

Except for THAT day; it was different. I felt different. I was made to feel different; different and unsure. "What did I do? Why were those kids angry? Kill? Who? When? Why?" It began a long period of questioning what it means to be different and why people do what they do to be hurtful to each other.

My searching has never really stopped. There are still lots of unanswered questions. I continue to get mad and sad at how we treat each other because of that word "different."

Somewhere the word UNIQUE began to seep into my consciousness. What if we were seen as unique rather than merely different? How would that change relationships? You know; the snowflake theory of no two alike, yet all beautiful.

UNIQUE became the starting point in my coaching sessions with executives and business teams. What are the talents and skills that can be used for positive results? How can the UNIQUE qualities in every one of us blend for more collaborative and effective work?

As I pondered how to create a method to explore human uniqueness I had an "aha" moment. Once we really can hear each other's stories, we begin to see each other in more compassionate ways. We look at each other from a new vantage point; we hear each other more clearly; it feels better.

I paid closer attention to the use of story at work. I knew the world of PowerPoints and statistics needed a more human dimension. I experimented with the ideas surrounding appropriateness of story and timing; what to say and the perfect time to say it.

I listened carefully to find the balance point between the indulgence of "too much information" and the denial of "no big deal." Now I was ready to help leaders add story to their list of skills. The use of story made a difference, every single time, no exceptions.

And from all the trials and tests to see what really mattered, SANKOFA Mapping™ was born! You will learn about the meaning of this "unique" word in Part One of this book. Everything will make so much sense when you learn the power of the word Sankofa and about the Sankofa bird, the wonderful symbol attached to it.

"People are hungry for stories. It is part of our very being." – Studs Turkel

This is a specific method of storytelling that helps you connect the dots of your life over generations. It is both a mental and emotional genealogy chart … that and so much more. It is like having a personal treasure map. I promise you it is worth exploring, so read on.

This book is for all who are in leadership positions, or aspire to be leaders … leaders interested in a people-oriented, productive bottom line. It helps leaders get underneath what separates us and causes gossip, backbiting, power games, and the burden of high stress.

It is a map to help you discover why certain people push your buttons while others are appreciated, even if they are saying basically the same thing.

It is a map that helps supervisors and work teams connect the dots of how to access the best in each other, to work together in a fulfilling and creative way; no exceptions.

It is for those in Human Resources whose mandate is to create beneficial diversity programs for their organizations. It is for team leaders who want to get underneath much of the superficial rhetoric about collaboration and see what does and can work long term.

It is what is needed for the 21st Century marketplace that is and will continue to be global. It is about a stronger and more durable foundation on which we can all stand strong and see each other in new and more positive ways.

SANKOFA Mapping™ is a power tool to help unlock potential for creativity and collaboration.

This book took shape long before I wrote the first word. It began when that first stone hit my body as a little kid and I was called names that made no sense to me, and then watched how the adults in my world took on the challenge of facing or avoiding the ugly world of diversity.

I watched my mother go into action. I heard her on phone call after phone call, getting very agitated, saying, "It is nonsense to shrug and simply say 'kids will be kids.' They need some adult attention so they don't carry

*this sort of behavior into the future and teach it
to their own children. Let's stop the spread of
hate now."*

*A meeting was set with the principals of
both schools. Parents attended, although not as
many as my mother would have liked. It ended
with the boys being chastised, requiring a
written apology to us.*

*Books were sent around for all the parents
to read and discuss with their sons and
daughters. Did they really follow through? Who
knows?*

The pattern of speaking up was programmed in my
young brain, the pattern of facing rather than avoiding or
denying. We are all taught at such an early age to model
the grown-ups in our lives, either to be open and willing
to address conflict or cover it over out of fear. I am
dedicating this book to my mother and to all the people
who have ever said, "It will stop with me."

The book is in three parts. The first is about the
power of observation. It is about the level of personal
awareness that you need to develop as a leader. It is about
learning to observe more effectively the daily interactions
that occur both at work and at home. You get the
opportunity, through the use of story, to see beyond the
obvious. And believe me, this can be a major relief.

You will gain clarity in answering the questions:
"Why do individuals often respond in ways that make no
sense?" or "Why do I always make the same mistake
over and over and over?" or "Why can't she stop blaming
others when she knows she plays a part in the dissention?"

It describes what happens when the SANKOFA
Map™ is used in leadership development to take you to a

deeper source of professional and personal growth; how self-discovery leads to compassion and creative ideas.

You will see what happens when stories are shared about how each of us was accepted or rejected for being "different" in a world that does not yet have a clear path to celebrating being UNIQUE.

At the end of each chapter in Part One there are questions to answer that will prime the pump for the rest of the learning in the book. Please take the time to answer them. It is better if you write down the answers so you can look back when you do the work of Part Two.

This next part gives you the tools to do your own SANKOFA Map™. This is the same process that is utilized in the second of our four-session Total Leadership Connections™ (TLC) program. Here you move to a new level of understanding the power of how the forces from family and culture are at play in your life right here, right now.

You can either explore your map with a certified SANKOFA Coach™ in a small group or one on one, which of course is highly recommended. However, even doing your map alone using the questions and suggestions in this book is still a very powerful and important process. It puts diversity training in a new light. This is where UNIQUE moves us beyond the statistics into a new realm of dialogue with each other.

You also get information on the 13 most common ingrained and outdated behavior patterns that show up in the workplace such as the procrastinator, the avoider, and the victim. These patterns from childhood bubble up when stress hits the hot button.

Once you see and understand how these familiar conditioned ways of responding jump out as protection devices, you can learn to tame them.

The third part of this book is all about trans-formation. Story plays a major role here by learning to

17

use what I call "The Goldilocks Method" of not too much and not too little. Here you learn to become a PatternAware Storyteller™.

Here you see how those patterns imprinted from your ancestral roots, which have become old and stale, can be turned to a new positive direction. You gain the ability, as a leader, to share targeted stories with others so they can also find the courage to search for their own patterns that may be steeped in unconscious bias.

Using story here is a wake-up call for direct reports and team members who have been afraid to show up fully or, conversely, become overly outspoken. In either case these extremes derail long-term success.

You are in a position to take diversity training to a new level of openness and authenticity without creating discomfort, by using the OUT Technique™ (Observe, Understand, Transform). Once you have gained the skill to observe and understand the generational patterns, you are ready to bring this vital information to your employees at work.

This information leads to more honest discussions, sparking new, effective ways of team consolidation. It is about the power of taking the PatternAware™ leadership and diversity model into the workplace and then watching the magic of transformation happen.

We are all different. Even better, we are all UNIQUE.

Let's have our special gifts stand center stage and not waste more time hiding from or fighting with each other. Join me in taking this leadership and diversity management resource-oriented model of working together to the next level of caring, sharing, collaboration, and productivity.

The overarching theme of this diversity work is … "We are all connected and no one wins unless we all do." In this flat and crowded world there really is no other way. My company, through its many programs, has helped large and small organizations, leaders, and teams find ways to honor diversity and create cultures of inclusion.

The philosophy of seeing each other as UNIQUE as well as connected, and extending a hand to our colleagues, has a lasting impact for years to come to transform organizations for the better in all work settings. http://www.ceoptions.com

Please turn to Part One and let's get started.

UNIQUE: How Story Sparks Diversity,
Inclusion, and Engagement

PART ONE: OBSERVE

We All Have a Story

"To be a person is to have a story to tell."
– Isak Dinesen

In this section you have an opportunity to see how the power of personal stories engages. Story, more than any formal presentation, opens a dialogue that creates valuable insights, innovative ideas, and new solutions both personally and professionally. When you hear others as they search for their roots, what came even before they or you were born, you develop the ability to observe the impact of the past on present workplace relationships.

Chapter 1: Different

A butterfly, flitting around the business convention, caught my eye and held me transfixed.

Everything else was winter brown and grey and dark blue, except for that orange and yellow swirl.

I was getting ready to start the workshop based on my book *GUTSY: How Women Leaders Make Change* and the butterfly landed in a seat near the back of the room.

I was fascinated.

I was curious about who she was and what gave her the courage to stand out from the crowd, at least in her choice of clothing. I wondered if that courage was more than cosmetic.

When she had an opportunity to speak I was not disappointed.

Kathleen had lived in Atlanta for several years, working and pursuing her MBA. After September 11, 2001, she and her husband decided to return to their homeland of Ghana to be closer to family. She made a vow to use her education to help bring leadership to her country.

As she spoke she smoothed her dress, did a pirouette, and said, "The women of my town made this dress for me to wear in America. They looked at American and French magazines and fashioned this dress in the beautiful, bright colors we love so much and made it in this modern style."

Sighs of approval came from the rest of the women in the workshop. Kathleen continued, "At first I was unsure about wearing this to a business meeting. And then I thought that if I am seen as different, so what? That happens to me all the time. I still feel the difference my very dark skin color makes in this country. And at home I am different because of my education."

Leadership is about being seen as UNIQUE, a one of a kind, to stand out from the crowd and make a difference.

Kathleen looked to see how she was being accepted as her next sentence flew out of her mouth in strong, vibrant tones. "What I want is to be seen as unique, a one of a kind. After all, isn't that what leadership is about? To stand out from the crowd and make a difference?"

With that Kathleen sat down.

And I knew I had just begun a journey to write my next book and that she would be a vital part of it.

The question formed, "How can we stop seeing each other as *different* and start seeing each other as *unique*?"

The two words are worlds apart, and unique is what the world needs now.

YOUR TURN:

Think of two or three ways you can be considered UNIQUE.

_____

_____

_____

Chapter 2: Minds Meet

My adventure with this beautiful butterfly had begun.

After the workshop we sought each other out. I had to know more and I sensed I held a piece for her life puzzle also.

While I did not have the courage or the beauty to stand out in a physical way, I was used to asking provocative questions that would often make others squirm.

There we stood, two women different in so many ways. Each seeing herself as unique; each wanting and willing to break down boundaries that separate, boundaries that keep us quiet, silent, from ever getting to know each other.

She told me of her town, Kumasi, maybe six hours on an often bumpy road from the capital of Accra.

She was a force in the community and yet she needed more ... more understanding of the role of leadership, the ways to get the people of her town to think in broader strokes. She still struggled as a woman in a male-dominated world and she wanted the tools to create cooperation.

I knew my next sentence would catch her. "I have a leadership program at my company called Total Leadership Connections™ and one of the aspects of the program is to do a SANKOFA Map™."

She grabbed my arm, grabbed my shoulders and began to hug me and jump up and down. There we were like two buoys bobbing in the Hudson River. She pulled me up and down and we jumped together as she said, "SANKOFA, SANKOFA; that is a word from my country."

"I know," I responded. "It means *heal the past to free the present.*"

"I KNOW too!" She was transfixed saying the word and laughing, never expecting anyone in this businesslike group to spill the word SANKOFA into the mix of corporate strategy lexicon.

"HOW," she demanded, "did you ever find that word and how in Heaven's name do you use it in a leadership program?"

I could feel a small crowd forming around us wanting to get a whiff of the delight we were experiencing.

Kathleen looked at me and said quietly, "This is a unique happening."

Unique; there it is again!

I told her about my leadership program I had been doing for more than a decade. In fact it was to launch on that day we all have engraved in our minds and hearts, September 11, 2001. The program began a month later.

What happened on September 11 made me even more determined to work with men and women from various organizations using what I had learned consulting with so many companies over the years. I knew there had to be a better way to relate to each other, and that we had to find solutions to the complex division that was wreaking havoc in our world of "for" or "against" each other.

I talked about how the program was based on "know yourself" before you can be an authentic and outstanding leader at work.

Individual shifts in awareness and attitude are at the foundation of great places to work.

It was clear from all the work I had done in the business world that the foundation of great places to work would come from individual shifts in awareness and attitude that are foundational and then imple-mented with knowledge and skills.

I told her about the diversity experiment at the heart of the program; about the risks and delights of living at the edge of the possible.

While a variety of diversity initiatives exist in companies, most are not getting to the essence of what makes us hold back from each other, what causes us to become polarized and frozen by those who are not like us.

Kathleen nodded and smiled. Her brows fur-rowed when she talked about being in Atlanta both as a black woman and as someone from a foreign country. It had not been a warming experience and she was glad to be back in her country where she was a variation on a theme in terms of color, yet unique as a personality.

She was dogged in learning how SANKOFA had traveled across the ocean to be used in America.

We sat down for a cup of coffee so I could paint the picture of how SANKOFA, this fascinating word from Ghana, came into my life.

YOUR TURN:

What are 4 images that you get when you think about "healing the past to free the present?"

_____
_____
_____
_____

Chapter 3: Wisdom from Africa

I told her about the day, years ago, when I heard about a film called *Sankofa.* The word itself was curious and beautiful. The film, about slavery and finding one's roots, was playing at a local art theater for a few weeks.

Phillip, the African-American Vice President of a pharmaceutical company who told us about the film, became emotional when he talked about the scene at the port where the once-free members of various tribes walked down a narrow tunnel – the point of no return – thinking they were going to another area of land to work and instead were put on ships headed for slavery.

I remember flinching, thinking about my people, the Jews, who in Germany were led to showers to wash. This was their point of no return, to be gassed to death.

Phillip's words brought me back to his story. His words were bitter when he said, "They were headed to America, the land of the free and the home of the brave." That is such a great branding tag line. However to me, it is just so much bullshit.

"*Sankofa,* the movie," he said, "was intense." He admitted sadly that it did not do for him what the word means; it did not "heal the past to free the present."

"However," he added, "it was a unique and artfully-done film that helped me at least look at my genetic roots." His history held a dark unknown past that he had recoiled from exploring. And yet he knew the anger and shame he still felt (although he certainly attempted to hide it) were holding him back personally and professionally.

Unique journey?

Was Phillip's journey more unique than mine? Was there a way we could all go back to heal the past to free the present?

Does the past really matter?

UNIQUE: How Story Sparks Diversity, Inclusion, and Engagement

Most of the diversity programs in organizations are filled with statistics and stay in the present time, looking at today and pointing to tomorrow. Most business coaching does the same. It is about today and tomorrow.

What about the past?

"The past is prologue." – Shakespeare

"Study the past if you would define the future." – Confucius

"Life can only be understood backwards; but it must be lived forwards." – Kierkegaard

"The past is never dead. It's not even past." – William Faulkner

"I know of no way of judging the future but by the past." – Patrick Henry

The one that kept ringing through my head was an Australian aborigine saying: "We carry our ancestors in our hearts and sometimes on our backs."

It sounded like Phillip was carrying his ancestors on his back and the burden was exhausting.

YOUR TURN:

What memory do you have about how something in your past still has power over the way you think?

_____

_____

_____

_____

Chapter 4: Feeling Different

I wondered what to expect the following weekend when my husband Herb and I went to the suburb at the far end of Philadelphia where the film was playing.

Once in the theater in Drexel Hill, we were surprised to see that we were the only Caucasians there. This was a relatively mixed area, the birthplace of comedienne Tina Fey. Yet the film was, after all, about the black experience of coming to America. Even so, why were there not more white-skinned people in the audience? Didn't we all have a shared experience of living in this land together?

The film was a well-done artistic piece by Haile Gerima who taught at Howard University. The storyline was about an African-American model on a photo shoot at Cape Coast Castle in Ghana.

Self-absorbed and paying attention to her looks she meets a mysterious man named "Sankofa" who helps to spiritually transport her to look at her roots.

In a trance state she sees her lineage and those who were kept at the Cape Coast Castle, slaves who were in holding dungeons. She learned of "the point of no return," the last walk to the ships to carry them across the Atlantic.

The film ended and there was silence.

Rather than run for the exit we were asked to stay and participate in a discussion about what we had just experienced.

Everyone sat and waited for someone else to begin.

I was extremely uncomfortable. I felt like an interloper, a voyeur who had no right to be there.

And yet, there I was!

Eventually someone called out that he was frustrated because Gerima was born in Ethiopia and not part of the diaspora. The man commented that Gerima really had no right to make a film that was not about his story.

There was applause.

In this hall of dark-skinned people the word diaspora sounded odd to me. It belonged to my heritage; it was the story of the Jews for thousands of years. I started to squirm in my seat. Why were they using "my word" from "my legacy"?

I was triggered by the fact that I really needed to get out of there. I was merely different and not at all unique.

My husband saw my concern, leaned over and said, "Breathe; this is not about you." I pulled myself back into the moment and listened. There was good discussion in the theater. I tracked the comments and waited. I knew I needed to speak out and was just looking, listening, sensing the right time.

> **While the slave ships sailed
> generations ago, those
> watching the film *Sankofa* felt
> they too were part of that
> long-ago journey and had also
> been "sold out."**

I listened to the hurt and pain and anger of people who, while they personally were not put on ships to sail away and be sold, felt they were, in some way, part of that long-ago journey. They felt they had been "sold out."

When there was a pause I stood up and brought my thoughts into words. "This is awkward for me, and I wonder if it is for others in this theater. As you can see, my husband and I are the only ones here who can be classified as white."

My heart was pounding and I felt embarrassed and wanted to retreat to silence and safety.

YOUR TURN:

When have you ever been the only one of your race or culture in a situation; and how did it make you feel?

_____

_____

_____

_____

Chapter 5: A New Kind of Acceptance

I stood there. I looked around and thought it best to just sit down again. It was too late. I had crossed the point of no return.

All eyes were in my direction. "This is different for me. It is a unique experience. I have never been the only white person, anywhere. I want to say I love the film and love the meaning of SANKOFA, to heal the past to free the present.

"And yet, on some level I feel like a voyeur, like I should not be here impinging on your privacy. I wonder how you feel about us being here. I will sit down now. I would appreciate hearing from any of you if you care to respond. And if you do not want to say anything, I understand."

What happened next is locked in my memory, in that place of "only a few moments like this in a lifetime."

The audience burst into spontaneous applause. People stood up and said "welcome friend" or "welcome neighbor" or "welcome sister and brother."

They asked me to speak about my experience both watching the film and being the only "whities" in the room.

It was an emotional time.

My usual love of words gave way to simple terms as I spoke of wanting to get a deeper understanding of the legacy of pain and shame from slavery in this country and how we are all sadly so mired in the thick goo of fear of how to appropriately discuss diversity and differences.

I also mused about what would have happened in that theater if it had been a program for whites with some token dark-skinned individuals there.

Those who remain silent about the abuses of the past are guilty too.

I thought about the word SANKOFA and the fact that healing the past belongs to all of us. I heard my daughter Mikayla Lev's voice when she had been filming with some inner city youngsters and told me about the song they wrote titled, "Those Who Remain Silent Are Guilty Too."

I did not know then that SANKOFA was calling to me, that it was to become a part of my world forever after that night.

Years later, Herb and I would go to visit the Elmina Castle near Kumasi with Kathleen and her husband. It was on a day when only two other people were there, young men from Germany exploring Africa.

We would talk about slavery and the multiple holocausts that wars present. We sat for long hours ignoring the hot sun as we, the six of us, wondered how long it would take for humanity to transcend the present crises all around the world. And I would walk down the dank corridor to the point of no return, getting a kinesthetic feeling of what it is like to throw joy and freedom to the winds.

YOUR TURN:

Think of a time when you were accepted, or not, for speaking out in an uncomfortable setting.

_____
_____
_____
_____

33

Chapter 6: Beginning the Connections

Kathleen stood looking at me, eyes wide like a child ready for a party. She must have sensed I had an idea that would change both of our lives, and especially hers, forever.

"How long are you going to be in the U.S.?" I asked. This was the beginning of a long and complex question.

"I plan to stay for at least several weeks. I have an uncle and cousin still in Atlanta and I will go visit them. Why?"

"Our next leadership program is starting in a week and I would like to invite you as my guest. However...," my voice trailed off, wondering if we would ever be able to make this four-session program work for someone from as far away as Africa.

"However," I continued, "this means coming back three more times and...."

"I will make it happen," she shouted. "Don't you worry! I am here to bring leadership training back to Ghana and any program that uses SANKOFA has to be the right one."

A week later, Kathleen from Kumasi, Ghana, showed up at our retreat center in Pennsylvania. She was one of fourteen participants in the four-session Total Leadership Connections™ (TLC) program. Her wide-eyed curiosity was infectious and she went from person to person to say hello as if she were running for political office.

Session one is always a mixed bag of openness and wariness. The group is purposefully small so no one can get lost at the periphery. The natural tendency for most in new settings is to protect oneself personally and yet still want to be noticed. This creates a palpable initial tension.

"Self-awareness is a vital aspect of leadership," says the TLC brochure. Yet the essence of self-awareness is experiential. You cannot intellectualize it, you have to feel it. And until the program gets underway this stays words on a page rather than meaningful to real life.

The new way of business, moving far from the Industrial Revolution of hierarchy, is collaboration. We are still learning how to do this. Hierarchy is just much easier. You do not have to listen, to deliberate; you just point your finger and say, "Do what I tell you to do."

Diversity management of the 21st Century requires deeper dialogues and more personal input.

While most companies want culturally-relevant training, the dilemma is the struggle between going into an uncharted territory of honest dialogue or keeping it safe and simple.

Diversity issues are anything but simple! They are complex and go to the very essence of how we learn to see the world as safe or not.

YOUR TURN:

What comments can you make about diversity training you have received in the workplace?

_____

_____

_____

_____

Chapter 7: Learning to TRUST

Underneath all leadership development programs is the challenge of how to get diverse individuals to learn to see each other as unique rather than merely different. Leaders are the organizational spark to make this happen, to spearhead the idea that there can be no tolerance for intolerance.

However, leaders first must look deeply into their own unconscious beliefs and assumptions and do some soul searching. For example, someone may be uncomfortable with a man wearing a "keppa" (Religious Jewish male head covering) or shy away from a man wearing a "tagiyah" (a cap worn by Muslim men), or dislike seeing a man wearing a "turban" (worn by Sikhs).

One type of headgear may instill a subtle level of fear. Another may be a symbol of "family." A piece of cloth is more than just some knitted or woven material when on someone's head. It comes to mean "just like me" or "stranger" or "enemy" and our emotions take hold as we go into acceptance, fight, or flight mode.

**It is dangerous and costly for
self-awareness and leadership
development to be separated.**

Our values and beliefs show up and will spill into our organizations in a myriad of ways. Those who are aware and able to observe their behaviors and respond according to what is best for the organization, for the situation at hand, rather than avoiding the issues are the leaders we need now more than ever.

The Total Leadership Connections™ group you are about to meet is comprised of fourteen people. The groups are meant to be small enough for lots of air time and connecting. You will hear the stories of a few of those who were there with Kathleen to give you an idea of how the personal storytelling part of the program works.

The 14 men and women in the present TLC group come from a wide variety of companies and back-grounds. Each is a CEO, president, vice president, or supervisor; and most have direct reports. The companies are as varied as the individuals. There are those from pharmaceutical companies sitting next to cement company engineers, media leaders, educational admini-strators, beauty and spa industry creative types, technology services innovators; and retailers from clothing to tires to automobiles are represented.

These individuals have been asked by their Boards or bosses or Human Resource representatives to hone their leadership skills and bring back to their respective business areas the key elements that make individuals and teams work together in the fluid and flexible economy of today.

It is not easy for any company to examine its existing culture and find new and effective ways for employees to relate in this ever-changing world. The knee-jerk reaction to "this is the way we have always done things" is still a constant and frustrating echo in the halls of commerce.

Change is hard. It takes unique men and women to make lasting change happen. There is cynicism in most organizations and much talk about the "flavor of the month" program that looks good, feels good, and yet has no lasting nutritional value over time.

Fact: Companies spend $5 billion per year on leadership programs.

Fact: Diversity programs do not lower the number of lawsuits that cost businesses $20B per year.

**Fact: High levels of stress-related illnesses
at work associated with bias of any kind
are on the rise and cost companies $10B
per year.**

Do the math ..... something is missing!!!!!!

The men and women in TLC have been chosen to
bring the learning back to their companies and implement
in ways to facilitate positive change for better
cooperation and collaboration, for productivity and prof-
itability.

The journey is complex.

It is not a traditional "sit and take notes" type of
program. It is experiential and requires consistent
participation. In this first of the four sessions there is
trepidation and caution. Everyone looks around wondering how the hell they ended up here.

Everyone in this group had that "rock in the pit of
the stomach" feeling ... everyone, that is, except
Kathleen. For she was finally going to find out how
SANKOFA came to America and how she could bring it
back to the country of its birth to help the nation of
Ghana become a leader in Africa.

YOUR TURN:

Describe your attitude and emotions when you have been
in a new workshop or new meeting and how you
processed the group.

_____
_____
_____
_____

Chapter 8: Snowflakes and Igloos

How many individual snowflakes does it take to make an igloo that will keep us safe in very cold weather? That is the challenge of getting a group to become a team. It takes time and focused effort.

That is what TLC is all about.

The first stop on the TLC train is getting the foundation about what it means to be a leader.

Session two goes into the world of SANKOFA that will be discussed in detail.

The third session brings us back into the present time to look at how our history plays out in all of our relationships. We learn to do a PEP Talks™ (Pattern Encounter Process) to see how to communicate in new and more effective ways.

The fourth session is when it is commitment time to make positive change in our work and personal lives.

In the fourth session Kathleen, as well as many others in the program, made some decisions that forever changed their lives.

More on that later.

Leadership has been much bandied about in the past few decades. Thousands of books and seminars focus on leadership and yet the constant cry is that we do not have many "real" leaders in the world of work, the world of education, and especially the world of politics.

In TLC there are more questions than answers, especially in this first session as individuals attempt to make sense out of the others in the group first, and then hopefully themselves.

Here is a snapshot of the 14 that had gotten on the TLC leadership train for the four-session program, each starting on Wednesday evening for dinner and completing on Friday morning by 11am.

UNIQUE: How Story Sparks Diversity,
Inclusion, and Engagement

This is not a personal growth seminar, a therapeutic workshop, nor a business program with a cookbook "how to" approach. It has been designed to show a unique way to blend personal and professional perspectives and find the balance point for extraordinary leadership.

This group of 14 along with Kathleen included:

1. Charles, who grew up in Taiwan and came to the U.S. at age seven. He is a VP in a medical technology company providing hospitals with tracking methods for patient files.

2. Scott, from a fourth-generation farming family who grew up in Sacramento, California, and is head of a sales team for an automotive supply franchise.

3. Jim, a physician, part Cherokee on his mother's side and Irish on his father's, who taught at Stanford Medical School and is presently on sabbatical before returning to the academic arena.

4. Anita, an African-American woman who is a lawyer in one of the big pharmaceutical companies.

5. Kevin, born outside of London, is head of accounting in the U.K. for a large international technology company.

6. Andrew, a bandana-wearing hairdresser from Texas, who left the military, where he was in Special Forces, to start a chain of highly-successful salons.

7. Mike, a physician who started his own medical device company and is about to acquire another company to double his revenue.

8. Eloise, brought up in South Africa, who lives in Arizona and owns an aesthetics and massage school.

9. Mariana, originally from Poland, a research scientist specializing in cardiology who heads a team at one of the largest pharmaceutical companies.

10. Ravi, who grew up in Chennai, India, and now lives with his family in Cleveland and is head of finance for a health care organization.

11. Ruth, African-American, originally from Mississippi, now head of Human Resources at a well-established clothing company in Man-hattan.

12. Ramon, whose family from Mexico migrated to San Diego, and is now the third-generation son to take over the presidency of the family construction business.

13 Kathleen, who is here from Kumasi, Ghana, to take leadership tools back to her town, her country, her people.

14 Martin, the most reluctant of the group. The CEO of a large retail organization, he insisted he was here just to "observe" to decide if this was right for his senior leadership team.

The first evening after dinner the program officially starts. It is a time for people to get to know each other and what is expected of them.

They are asked to tell a bit about who they are and what they hope to get from the program. Many simply told the basics, sort of a name, rank, serial number mentality. Others shared mainly about their business track record. A few talked about family with minimal details, as in how long married and how many children.

**What does it take to move from a
survival mentality to one where
we can be authentic and open to
thrive instead of just survive?**

Everyone stays careful. Each gives just enough information to remain a unique and separate snowflake. The igloo concept, how they would become stronger together, would have to wait until later. This is how groups start, not just at our program but at most programs.

It is vital to create safety; and that is one of the most important skills of a leader, of a facilitator, to make it safe enough to learn.

Without safety there is a tendency to remain suspicious, cautious, and protective. We are programmed to survive; and to survive we need to know the rules of the game we are asked to play.

And yet, are we not ready to get past survival to a new level of thriving? That is the question!

At first blush this was a group, like most, that would learn the rules and then speak out. The evening was drawing to a close; and yes, it was following protocol. Everyone followed the unwritten rules to play it safe and wait to see what happens.

Everyone, that is, except one.

YOUR TURN:

Think of a time when you did not play it safe; and what were the ramifications?

_____

_____

_____

_____

Chapter 9: New Rules for the Old Game

Right as we were ready to end the evening meeting, Mike asked for the floor.

I said an inner prayer that he was reading the group properly and would wait. That what he wanted to say was some pleasantry and that would be it. It was, my tired mind said, too soon for full disclosure.

I heard my inner voice caution Mike, "Careful. Remember we teach that *telling the truth is not spilling your guts.*"

And then all I could do was hope I would not have too much damage control to handle at this late hour.

Mike was bright, well-educated, and now very wealthy. He was the CEO of his company and had lots of direct reports. Before he joined this leadership program he asked for private time with me. He wanted to make sure his "secret" would not interfere with the learning for the whole group.

He wanted to really probe into the issues of diversity and inclusion and was not sure this would be the place. I assured him it was. I assured him that those who joined this program were the kind who wanted to live "on the edge of possibilities" and were interested in the art as well as the craft of leadership.

I suggested he trust his intuition to decide when it would be the right time to share his secret. I would not be the tale barer. His secret was his to tell in as much or as little depth as he chose.

So, here we were at the end of a long evening, ready for wine and cake and comfort talk before bed. And here was Mike wanting to keep the conversation going.

Sometimes the most important part of a conversation comes in the last three minutes.

While I really wanted to stop him, to say "not now," there was a curiosity in the room that would not be denied. Those who had started to close their notepads and turn their cell phones back on sat down.

The moment came sooner than I preferred and yet, there it was. I know that each group has its own personality, just as individuals have ways of being with others, of responding at an invisible level we call the subconscious or even more aptly, the unconscious.

A major part of leadership is learning to read the signs of what is NOT being said in a group and to know when to prod and when to leave situations alone. Great leadership is, as we teach, "all in the timing." More often than not there is superficial politeness about sharing real feelings when a group forms and it is best left that way initially.

When the norm is broken it must be tended to immediately.

I heaved a sigh to release the tension that was building in my body and turned to Mike.

"What would you like to say?"

And from that moment I knew we were going to enter a new realm of discussing diversity and inclusion. The concepts of different and unique were going to be dissected and put back together in ways I could not yet imagine.

Mike stood. I so wished he had stayed seated. Standing would only make what he was about to say more dramatic.

"I, Mike, have only been half truthful. Yes, I am a physician. Yes I have just acquired a second company,

44

and yes I have made a great deal of money in my career. No, I am not bragging. You see I left out the most important piece of talking about who I am."

He took a breath and looked over at me. I merely nodded for him to continue. The cat was already half out of the bag.

"I, Mike, was born into a family as the third and youngest child of Renee and David Levy. Obviously you can get that I was born Jewish. That is not such a big deal to me, although it does carry some emotional burdens."

If Mike dragged this out much more the room was about ready to burst and so was I. Some figured that he was going to admit that he was gay. Others later told me they thought he was going to say he was a "Jews for Jesus" member.

One more sentence was all that was needed.

"You see, I was born Marilyn. Marilyn Levy. I was a cute little girl. Except something didn't compute, and three years ago I finally became who I was meant to be and Marilyn became Mike.

"So there you have it and now I do not have to pretend. I have no idea how each of you will respond to me. I do know, however, that if we are going to go on this diversity journey together I have to play full out. Talk about diversity. I hit lots of buttons. I am Jewish, I was of the female gender, I am now in that lowly category of white male, and I am transgender. I guess I hit the diversity jackpot."

The room was achingly silent.

He continued, "If this is too much for all of you I can gracefully leave the group tonight."

All eyes were now on me.

Different, unique, similar, familiar; does it really matter if he is Mike or was Marilyn? What really does matter on this journey of leadership, of life? How do we hold the space for individual differences and how do we create teams that can respect each other, get along, and work together?

Lots of questions and not the time for answers; it was too soon. I honestly wished he had waited until the group had created a sense of safety.

He didn't wait and now this had to be tended to.

YOUR TURN:

How do you handle uncomfortable situations?

_____

_____

_____

_____

Chapter 10: Does the Truth Set Us Free?

The reactions were as varied as the designs that snowflakes make. Some smiled politely. Others were looking down at the floor. A few were literally rolling their eyes in consternation for what was just said.

Why did this man/woman have to share his secret? It was no one's business. Why did he have to tell? No one had asked.

I was used to complex situations, although this one on a scale of 1-10 registered about a 13. I took the internal pulse of the room before I spoke.

"And so we have begun. Mike took a risk to tell the truth about who is he." I looked in his direction and nodded before I continued. "He did not have to say a word. So, the questions are … Why would he speak out in a group? Why would he speak out in a business program? What is the upside of telling the truth? What is the downside? These are deep and important questions that all leaders must grapple with. Tomorrow we will take the next step into the land of leadership. For tonight we will hold up on more discussion. It is late. So, Mike, I just want to check; if anyone wants to talk with you personally where would you like to talk?"

Mike thanked the group for listening and said he would be in the library area. "It's a quiet place to talk for anyone who wants to know more."

Kathleen asked Mike if he would like some coffee and said that she would bring it and she definitely wanted to meet with him. Several others nodded they would like to meet also. The rest fired up their phones and started to check e-mails or call home.

And I said to myself once again, "And so we have begun."

Mike pulled me aside, having second-guessed himself. He looked concerned. "Hey Sylvia, was that out of line? Did I ruin the program already? You see, you and only a few others including my family and my girlfriend know, well knew about me until tonight. I just felt impelled to say something and not hold back. Maybe it was too much."

We were, as Mike realized, on thin ice. So much of the territory of sharing who we are and what our lives are about is kept behind closed doors, especially in the workplace. There are no easy answers; and this group, early in the program, now had an opportunity to learn how to navigate this mostly-uncharted terrain.

Opening up the locked closets where truth often resides is risky and liberating.

We were NOT in a group therapy program and this is NOT reality television. Any leadership program that begins with self-awareness will certainly have therapeutic results; yet learning to navigate the interface of personal and professional disclosure is tricky. "Maybe," I said to Mike, "just maybe you opened the door in this group to discover a faster track to truth.

"Mike, everyone has some type of secret. Secrets have a way of outing; and in this case you are in charge of, not at the effect of, telling your truth on your terms. This will help us see how strong we are and how willing we are to respond to each other in new, more effective ways. You are both different and unique. Let's focus on the unique. Tomorrow is another day."

Mike met with three others and I waited to see who needed to discuss what happened with me. When no one showed up I grabbed my cup of tea and headed for my bedroom.

"Tomorrow," I said to myself, "should be challenging and worthy of at least an article for *Harvard Business Review*."

I fell asleep wondering what it would be like if I had chosen to change to a man's body.

YOUR TURN:

When faced with situations that go against your belief system what do you do?

_____

_____

_____

_____

Chapter 11: Fear and Avoidance

One man did ask to see me privately at breakfast. It was Scott. He was a tall handsome man, and from what I heard he was also a super salesperson. He made lots of money for his company and he was here to be groomed for a senior V.P. position and begin working globally.

"Sylvia, I did not sleep much last night. I decided I want out of this program and I would like to leave now rather than disrupt the group later. I am just not comfortable with what happened last night. Now don't get me wrong. Whatever that guy/gal did in his/her life is really none of my business. I just do not think he/she should have said anything."

Scott's comments were familiar: ignore and deny. That was the way most people prefer to handle the discomfort of conflict. He continued, "I would never have guessed that Mike had been born Marilyn; and now that I know, I honestly do not know how to talk with him/her. Look, I do not have any deep secrets and even if I did, this would not be the place to talk about them. I just want to learn how to be effective in dealing with a global sales force. This is just too personal for me. So as that old John Denver song goes, *my bags are packed and I'm ready to go.*"

I let what Scott said sink in. Part of me was so willing to have him leave. It would be easier for the group if he left and took his fear with him. And yet, if I gave in too easily, what would be learned about the virus of fear and how it spreads from one to another, especially when we have to face differences head on?

I asked Scott to at least give it until lunchtime; and if he still felt this was not right for him, he could tell the group and leave.

He nodded reluctantly and went to get some coffee.

50

It was a crapshoot if Scott would find something positive and let his curiosities about change win, or if his fear of another would lead him out the door.

The morning was crammed full of discussions about effective listening, how to ask engaging questions, and the art of meeting facilitation, the black hole of the business world.

Mike had settled into his role as a wise and fun individual and the group was seeing him as the man he had become not the little girl he once was.

I kept glancing at Scott, wanting to read his mind and wanting to convince him to stay. Yet I had to let go of what I would prefer and permit life to take its course.

As we walked to the dining room Scott called me aside and stated in a strong voice that he would be leaving. He said his religious beliefs would get in the way and this was just not the learning setting that would be best for him.

He felt that Mike was going against God's plan and he did not want to bring this up with the group. He asked if I would simply tell the others he had a business emergency and he would go and pack and make a quiet exit.

"No," I said, and saw the look of displeasure cross this tall man's face. I did not challenge him to stay, telling him only to say what he thought was appropriate for what I have come to call "honorable closure."

"Scott, I cannot speak for you and I know it is always easier to avoid discomfort. However, you came here to learn more effective leadership skills and at least you can leave with dignity. Take the task of leaving a tough situation in the best way possible."

Scott became angry. "Damn it, Sylvia, you knew he was transgender. Why did you ever let him into this program? He may be a physician or call himself one. I see him as a freak of nature, a biological travesty against all that God stands for."

There are no words to argue with someone when they have blinders on, caught in their own circle of upset. The best I could hope for was that he would not spill his venom into the room. His beliefs were deeply instilled, and in my mind I kept hearing the Rogers and Hammerstein song from *South Pacific*:

You've got to be taught to hate and fear
You've got to be taught from year to year
It's got to be drummed in your dear little ear
You've got to be carefully taught

Scott left with a lie. He told the group that something had come up at home with his young son who had an accident and he needed to get back to help his wife. He wished the group well and "would join another program at a later time." And with that he was like a ghost, vanishing from our lives.

Everyone sensed the lie and felt Scott's conflict with what had happened. Mike spoke up. "I guess it was my fault. I did speak too soon. Maybe I should have kept quiet. It really is no one's business."

The room was silent.

The irony is we were ready to do an outside experiential process, a trust walk.

How perfect.

The trust walk is where half the group is blindfolded and they have a sighted partner who leads them through the wooded area outside.

I had this crazy thought I did not share with the group. I wondered what Scott would have done if he had stayed and somehow was physically hurt and the only doctor around was Mike. Would he have said, "No, leave me in my pain!" or accept the help that I know Mike would have given him?

Here is an even more impossible setting, one of those "truth is stranger than fiction" scenarios. Three years later Scott called and in a quiet voice asked if he could participate in the next TLC group. Fate had stepped in. Scott and his daughter had been in a devastating car accident and both were now physically challenged. His daughter was a paraplegic in a wheelchair for life and he had, as he attempted to joke, a "gimp leg."

Life had softened him. "I am still working and I want to make a difference for everyone with disabilities. I need to find my voice. Can you help?"

A very different Scott joined a new group and learned about the power of story and connection.

YOUR TURN:

What beliefs do you have that are non-negotiable, and how do you handle situations where you are required to stay or leave?

_____

_____

_____

_____

Chapter 12: Small Steps

Building trust is a complex issue.

It can start by having someone take your hand when you are blindfolded and the powerful sense of sight is taken away, albeit briefly. You are beholden to another and to their hopefully good intention of doing no harm. It is not so different from being a child in a parent's arms. You can only hope they will be careful and have your best interests at heart.

And what is the process of building trust with someone you see as "different"?

This is the grand experiment: black and white, male and female, gay and straight, evangelical and atheist, Muslim and Jew, boomer and millennial, and on and on; so many categories of difference.

We learn to sort at an early age. We put all the circles together, the squares with the squares, and the triangles in a neat pile. We are told that is good; except, we cannot make really great designs without a mixture of all of them.

Helping people trust someone they view as "different" means finding a shared language, a common denominator to move situations forward.

Every team-building program I have led has many similar elements. Initially when the group is asked what they want to accomplish by the end of the session, every … and that is *every* group … always wants to develop more trust.

**How do we know when it is
safe enough to trust? We
cannot see it nor measure it;**

and yet, when it is there we
KNOW it.

Trust, like love, is amorphous. It is an abstraction that you cannot see, and yet you know it when it is present. Trust, like love, is built on truth, and that truth is from the heart.

SANKOFA demands that we connect the mind and the heart in the search for the truth. This elegant word whispers for you to heal the past to free the present. You are asked to see how family, culture, and crises such as wars or early deaths live on through us.

The mythological SANKOFA BIRD is ready to come into the arena of business and make a difference. This bird can do what no other bird can. It can turn its neck backwards. This bird turns to pick up something on its back. It is an egg.

Why would a bird from ancient times turn around and pick up an egg? What meaning does it have for us today?

The egg symbolizes fertility, the life force that was left in the past, left "back there." The SANKOFA BIRD is taking that life force, that energy still able to be used, taking it in its beak and bringing it into the present where it can be nurtured and developed.

Heal the past to free the present is fraught with meaning for all of us.

Part of our evolutionary responsibility is to become observers of the patterns from the past that are still part of the present. Our responsibility is to decide which patterns from the past serve us and release the rest.

We are no longer bound to be at the mercy of what has been handed to us through generational ties. Our obligation is to heal, heal the past so the present is free for creative purpose.

UNIQUE: How Story Sparks Diversity, Inclusion, and Engagement

Loyalty, as most of us experience it, is to the past. A major component of war and prejudice involves invisible loyalties to family, race, nation, and religion. As we explore the past we can keep what still has health and is positive. Then we let the rest go and become free of the ties that bind and our loyalties are also freed. We can become loyal in new and positive ways and create a future that sustains life.

SANKOFA shows the wonder of an ancient icon and a profound meaning put into just that one word.

All ancient cultures were highly conscious of the impact of the past on the present. Chief Seattle addressed generational responsibility in his famous speech of 1851 when he responded to a proposed treaty under which the Native Americans were persuaded to sell several million acres of land around Puget Sound.

His speech states:

> *"You must teach your children that the ground beneath their feet is the ashes of our grandfathers. So that they will respect the land, tell your children that the earth is rich with the lives of the kin. Teach your children what we have taught our children that the earth is our mother. Whatever befalls the earth befalls the sons of the earth. If men spit upon the earth they spit upon themselves."*

Hard words and yet we have not heeded the ancient cultures that asked us to show respect to all that has come before and to take the time to heal the past to make way for the present.

SANKOFA Mapping™ is a modern way to take something ancient and bring it into our time. In older cultures, looking at one's life to decide what really

*"Even though the house is quiet and shut,
even though I am not in it, I am in it, and …
good-bye, you who are walking without
turning your head!"*

The SANKOFA BIRD is gently requiring you to turn around, to stop walking without turning your head and look back to find what was left and bring it into the present time.

YOUR TURN:

What are several facts you know from your heritage and what are some you want to learn about?

_____
_____
_____
_____

matters would be called "warrior work." In today's vernacular it is called leadership training.

Doing one's own SANKOFA Map™ is an active, participatory tool for leadership development. Before we can lead "out there" it is imperative to know what the forces are that are driving us internally.

YOUR TURN:

What are some basic beliefs that you teach or want to teach to the next generation?

_____
_____
_____
_____

Chapter 13: The Map to the Treasure

Like the Myers Briggs Personality Type Indicator and the Enneagram, both used in business settings around the world, the SANKOFA Map™ is a valuable tool for learning where the "knots" are still causing patterns of behavior responses to be stuck and how to change them for the better.

First you can take the PatternAware™ Quiz which is located at http://sylvialafair.com/pattern-aware-quiz/ to get a quick view of the behavior patterns that are deeply embedded from childhood. You will find 13 of the most common patterns learned at home that we bring to work.

Then the deeper dive is into the SANKOFA Map™ for the powerful learning about how these patterns have tumbled from generation to generation and which ones have landed in our specific laps.

**When we are alert to
why certain people and
situations push our buttons
we, not they, are in charge
of best ways to react.**

We all have certain situations, certain people who "push our buttons." Learning to observe those times, understanding where they developed, and having the courage to transform the way we respond to the button-pushing is a major part of leadership training.

The specific form for doing your own personal SANKOFA Map™ is in Part Two of this book. Before you plunge ahead it is good to get the hang of it by hearing some of the stories of those who have already completed their journey back home.

Ruth was the first to volunteer to be "it." She w to "get it over with"; and furthermore, since she was of Human Resources in her company, she deci would be best to see how it felt to do this presen and then decide if it was worth the time fo organization.

Utilizing the SANKOFA Map™ for charting personal and cultural flow of life gives an opportu look at the gifts as well as the challenges that handed to us.

Initially, many see only the dysfunctions, the and fear that was handed from generation to gene In doing the SANKOFA Map™ the individual s come together, the deep colors of grief or anger with the lighter ones of happy days for a tapestry its own diversity and beauty.

Today is Ruth's turn to stand at a flip cha present her family to a group of her peers. It is no thing to stand, in a manner of speaking, naked at warts and all. There is nothing more personal, sacred, and more filled with primal energy and po unutilized creativity than looking at one's family in a vast panorama.

This is no dry report filled merely with dat names. It is not a ledger of who begot who. It essence of who we have become, of how our pe ities have taken shape, of how our hopes and have manifested or fallen into stagnation, of how w come to embrace or expel each other.

Through our outer families, we have create inner families, the ones we take with us for the rest lives even if we choose to never see our outer fa again.

Poet Juan Ramon Jimenez states the power inner memories in *A Remembrance Is Moving* wh says eloquently:

Chapter 14: Looking Through New Eyes

Ruth is ready, albeit filled with trepidation. She began with a quote from *Gentlemen's Agreement*, a best-selling novel by Laura Hobson and Academy Award-winning film from 1951 about anti-Semitism.

"There is no more important work than beating down the complacency of essentially good people."

And so, not knowing where this exploration of her own life through the SANKOFA Map™ would take her and what it would mean to be witnessed by others, she was ready to dive in. The group was curious and the room was filled with nervous anticipation.

It is important to note that doing this map of your family and culture is part of a larger process. It is not a check-the-box project to do and be done with. The SANKOFA Map™ is, as has been said, a way to get to the buried treasure each one of us has inside. Then there is always an action plan on next steps. Without the action plan this is merely an academic exercise and will not have the real and powerful results it is meant to have.

This is not dinner talk about whether your mother or father or siblings were great to you or annoyed you to death. This is not about who was the most perfect or awful. It is not merely about the cultural norms that were part of the family dynamics. It is about the patterns that have tumbled from generation to generation and are still alive today.

I want to underline that we have found this type of work is best done in groups that do not work together on a daily basis, where individuals from various companies join together so that there is absolute safety and, for want of a better word, diversity.

UNIQUE: How Story Sparks Diversity, Inclusion, and Engagement

Ruth was one of the two African-Americans in the group. We sat in a room we could call "Little America," a microcosm of the macrocosm. Much of the diversity was obvious. Black, White, Asian, Hispanic, female, male were easily defined. Religion and nationality less obvious were touched upon with some insecurity. Gender issues about being gay and lesbian are just now beginning to be discussed; and Mike took us up a notch with transgender issues.

The room was filled with the ultimate human dilemma: how to handle concerns and insecurities that were part of the embedded patterns in each of us. There was a sense of desire to grow beyond old ways, and yet there was the fear of leaving the familiar.

Our stories are both personal and universal, and in sharing them we help each other grow.

Ruth's narrative was, in many respects, everyone's story. It was a story of unlimited hopes and relinquished dreams, of hugs and hurts and betrayals and courage. The actors in Ruth's personal play were uniquely hers, the themes universal.

Ruth related a story her mother had shared recently. It was a story sprinkled with laughter, tinged with bitterness, and laced with sadness.

Ruth had to "go home again" to gather information for her SANKOFA Map™. She admitted surprise at how much personal healing had taken place on the way to complete the map she pointed to now. It was no longer just circles and squares and dates, it was alive and pulsating with memories.

Ruth had harbored deep resentment toward her mother for all the yelling and arguing she had experienced as a youngster. She vowed NEVER to be like her mother and grew into a quiet, reserved woman who rarely voiced her opinion and felt that any type of arguing was crude.

She had remained an aloof grown daughter, and any talk at family gatherings stayed superficial. She refrained from being alone with her mother as much as possible.

Her mother, she told the group, was now in her late eighties and was suspicious and cautious when Ruth came to visit, alone. "It was awkward and I began to doubt the reasons behind doing this map. I did not want to upset my mother in these her golden years."

"I started to do my old just stay in the surface talk until my mother said, 'Ruth, you never visit without your husband and sons. And you are acting peculiar. If you have something to say to me, just say it. Who knows how long I will be around to answer your questions? After all I am 87 years old and you never know how long those complicated machines called lungs and heart will keep going.'"

Ruth started by asking her mother what it was like to be a little girl in a rural town in the South before Rosa Parks ever sat in the front of that bus.

Then the magic happened.

Ruth's mother permitted the gates to that traumatic childhood that had been padlocked to open. She shared with her daughter the shame of the little seven-year-old who had to walk over a mile to her school. She had to walk right past the white school where the kids would shout "nigger" and throw orange peels at the small band of youngsters walking by.

"I would tell my mother, your grandmother who died when you were a little bitty thing, what happened and she would look sad and say, 'Just pay them no mind. Character matters more than color and you got character.'

"Ever since then I became a fighter. I swore I would never let anyone see me cry and I have never cried a tear to wet my face since then." And yet, at that moment the elder woman's cheeks were glistening and wet.

Tears are the part inside that was frozen beginning to defrost.

Ruth, barely audible, reported to her leadership group that at that moment she saw her mother for the first time. She no longer saw the angry woman she detested. She saw the little girl whose blackness made her vow to be strong and that meant to hide her feelings.

Ruth brought the group with her as she painted the picture of when, at that moment, she put her hand on her mother's arm. Then the grown daughter and aging mother let the sweet taste of salty tears heal the years of distance.

YOUR TURN:

What are some of the prejudices you grew up with and how do you think about them now?

_____

_____

_____

Chapter 15: Connecting the Dots

During the next few weeks, post-SANKOFA Mapping™, Ruth e-mailed the group, encouraging each one to "give it a go, no matter what." She had, surprisingly, become stronger. She realized that while she became upset when people at work pushed the racial issue under the rug, she had done the same thing.

It was astounding.

Prejudice took on a whole new meaning. She had not faced her own deep prejudice against her own mother for not being the way she wanted her to be. She saw the roots of prejudice from a wider perspective.

She now knew that her human resources team had a lot of work to do to help her company make positive and appropriate changes in the way they handled "that diversity issue."

Over the intervening months, her relationships at work and also at home blossomed. She would call her mother every week and the woman at the other end of the line began to laugh and tell jokes and talk about what she was watching on television.

What also stood out was that while Ruth had been so determined to be the opposite of her mother, she had paid a   high price. She would not permit her teenage sons to spar with each other; and when her husband and sons wanted to handle disagreements with a great deal of noise she would intervene and stop the flow of the discussion.

Sometimes thinking you are the opposite is really just being stuck at the other end of the continuum.

She learned that this is called "polarized fusion" and it means that when we are stuck in a pattern we often go to the opposite; yet, we are still bound to the "NOTS" and this keeps us in "KNOTS."

Mike asked to go next. He needed to understand how his change of sexual identity would impact his work life moving forward.

On the surface, his background was a total opposite from Ruth.

He came from a well-to-do Jewish family living in a Jewish neighborhood on Long Island. Schools were closed on Jewish holidays and the synagogue was a meeting place for the children as well as the parents.

His growing up years were idyllic, except….

He never felt quite right. He hated playing with dolls, learning to cook, and how to be cute. He was, by most standards, a "pretty" little girl and did his best to fit in, except….

There were no words for his kind. He was always on the outside looking in. He had two older brothers, and being the "girl in the family" made it complete.

Time went on and he felt himself move into a world of books and study. He was talented in math and science and when he announced in high school he wanted to go to medical school his parents spent time trying to convince him it would be just fine to be a nurse or a teacher … a better life for a girl.

He dated boys and when it came to practicing "the kissing game" he said it gave him a gut reaction of wanting to vomit.

The group sat transfixed. Several had gay friends but this was on another level completely; and Mike, being the observer scientist, was able to take them to see this dilemma from new dimensions.

He knew he was not a girl wanting a gi was way more than that. He was in the wrong bouy. Someone, he joked, had slipped up on the order.

Mike walked the group through as many questions as he could answer about the operations to help him go from Marilyn to Mike.

Suddenly there was more room for understanding and acceptance.

Mike was on a hero's journey into uncharted territory. There were many others in the room who felt they too were alone on their paths. The specifics were different, the underlying emotions the same. Most stuffed their real feelings, and kept silent, until now, that is.

Chastity Bono, daughter of Sonny and Cher is now Chaz, Jeff Pritzker from the Hyatt family is now Jennifer; and as more well-known people speak out, shame begins to diminish.

Just a note to fast-forward to session four when Kevin, the buttoned-up accountant from London, who talked about being "plain vanilla emotionally," asked to speak. Until that moment he had, as he told us, "minimal problems, no real concerns, and wanted to just check the boxes of life and let the days pass uneventfully."

He spoke up with a passion that was so unlike his typical manner. "I don't know what I would have done if I had not been in this program right now. In the last few months between sessions the unimaginable happened."

Everyone sat up with images of drugs and sex and all kinds of awful, unimaginable happenings in gentle Kevin's life.

"You know I am an only child of an only child and that I have an only child, a good boy who is on his way to university next year. He has been a joy to my wife and me; and honestly, as I listened to so many of your situations I always felt like an outsider. Even when I did my SANKOFA Map™ I felt I had disappointed all of you, and myself, because I did not have much to say that was in any way dramatic."

We all still sat staring, wishing Kevin would just say it.

"However...," he paused, his manner so very English. I made a mental note wondering if others were thinking about the cultural stereotype or just reminding themselves of his early childhood training to not make waves. He needed to set the stage before jumping in the way the "brash" Americans do. Someone took the moment to deflect the tension by saying "Hey, Kev, go ahead; be a 'brash' American, just try it on for size."

The laughter helped. Kevin paused again, and looked around to make sure what he was going to say would be accepted.

Kevin told how that one precious son getting ready to go to university dropped the bomb on his parents that he is gay and could no longer hide the fact from them.

"Before this program," Kevin looked around at everyone, "I would have most likely created a great big wall between myself and my son. Being gay is just not acceptable in my family and I would have felt he betrayed me, and I know our relationship would have been superficial and flat from then on.

"Now I was able to talk with him and with my wife who was also ready to disengage from our son, and find a way to see life from a fuller perspective. He is a wonderful young man; and last week we all took another risk and he introduced us to his friend with whom he had shared an intimate relationship for the past year."

Kevin looked more alive, more open. "A secret has been ousted. Life is richer and fuller than it has been, well, forever."

With an uncharacteristic twinkle Kevin added, "I am really talking to all the blokes at work who are not like me. Guess I have missed half the world until now."

YOUR TURN:

When have you ever had to "change your mind" about a person once you have heard their story?

_____

_____

_____

_____

Chapter 16: Testing the Limits of Vulnerability

Vivian was the suburbanite of the group. Always well-coiffed and dressed in designer clothes she, of everyone, looked like she had grown up with a silver spoon for her cereal.

The day before she was to do her SANKOFA Map™ she called me wondering if maybe too much exposure could be damaging to her career and how the group would relate to her.

"You see, Sylvia," she said softly, "I know how I appear to others and I love the fact that I am considered the one who has it all together. I am a great leader at work and am here because I will soon take over the senior leadership of the marketing team. They just want me to be a bit more of a strong-armed general when I get there.

"I really wonder how vulnerable we need to be in front of others and how much of our life story is appropriate to tell."

By the time Vivian and I finished our conversation I was wondering the same thing. Should she tell of her trauma from childhood to this group? I began to have some self-doubt about the need to disclose what is super personal. Maybe I was barking up the wrong tree, and vulnerability and truth have limits.

That night I was in a perpetual dream state, more like a nightmare, as I lived through what Vivian told me. The anguish and pain of what so many innocent children have to deal with had me enraged by the time I awoke as the first shreds of morning light came streaming through the corners of the window shades.

The answer is always in the entire story, not in just a piece of it.

Vivian and I had agreed that she would have to decide as she was talking about her family tree if she felt safe enough to tell the whole truth. I was curious and wary, and also wondered how others would react to this very polished and senior woman who works in a prestigious Fortune 500 company.

Vivian glanced at me and nodded. She was going to "heal the past to free the present" and would let the truth take her wherever it would.

She was ready to be an example of a strong woman who would no longer stay in the background of life, on any level.

"My father," she said proudly, was a well-known PhD mathematician." She looked around the room. "Who here has seen the film *A Beautiful Mind?* Well, that was just like my father.

"He was head of the math department at one of the Ivy League schools and we always had these super-intellectual nerdy types come over for dinner and they would discuss in the language of mathematics that sounded like gibberish to us kids and always ended with 'Aha I never thought of it that way before.'

"To the world out there all was picture perfect. Except at night I would cringe in my bed waiting for the door to open and for him to disrobe and have sex with me. It went on from the time I was eight until I was thirteen when I finally was strong enough to push him away.

"I know you are all wondering why I didn't tell my mother or someone. I did tell my mother once and she simply patted me on the head and said it must have been a bad dream."

Everyone in the room began to squirm and I wanted to stop everything and, like Vivian's mother, pretend that it was really just a dream she was talking about.

I looked around the room and saw that she was truly in charge. Her story had power and her intent was to complete and heal rather than judge and blame.

Vivian went on to talk about the relief she and her two sisters along with their mother felt when her father was finally taken to the psychiatric hospital and a semblance of normalcy reigned at home.

"I have had years of therapy and that has helped. However, this SANKOFA Mapping™ is a new experience and what is amazing me is seeing my father in his lineage where there had been physical abuse and seeing how he and my mother got together because she grew up in an impoverished family where they were all victims too afraid to open their mouths about anything. He could dominate and she would acquiesce. She was just grateful he made a good living and she never had to worry about food on the table."

One of the most important aspects of being in a SANKOFA Mapping™ session is that we are not there to be therapists. We are there to listen, to ask open-ended questions, and learn about how patterns from our history show up at work and what to do to transform those patterns.

First we are there to gain insight into ourselves and then into others. The key is to find that unique spark in each one and then, as a leader, learn to fan that spark into a flame taking that uniqueness to its brightest place.

Vivian was able to see that where she had created a pattern at work was that she had early decided she could never trust anyone who was super smart, male or female, and felt that sooner or later she would be betrayed in some way. She steered away from some of the best and the brightest and it was like draining energy from her team.

Once we can observe a pattern that we repeat and repeat, it no longer has power over us.

She was also keenly aware that she was a pleaser who would hide discontent at any cost. No one was to ever know she had secrets and so she stayed superficial and sweet.

That had kept her from collaborating with some of the best minds in the company and now she saw this with laser-like clarity.

The group took a long break after Vivian's presentation and she sought me out wondering if she did the right thing. "Did I reveal too much? Was it one of those times I did not listen to the idea that 'telling the truth is not spilling your guts'? I wonder if I should have kept most of this in my secret place."

"Let's just see how the deeper connections show up during the remainder of our time here," I said.

My experience has been that after SANKOFA Mapping™ a deep bond is formed. There is true camaraderie. Sharing at this level is unique and doing it with the end result to become better leaders is the common denominator. All see each other as heroes on the journey of self-awareness.

The personal and universal aspects of each individual story have a powerful and positive effect and it has been reported over and over that back at work direct reports and colleagues are viewed with more compassion. Even if the "story" is never told, the fact that, of course, there is a "story" becomes clear. Individuals are seen in the richness and fullness of their multi-dimensional selves, not as characters from an insignificant sitcom.

Again, I want to underline that I would never suggest this type of process with an intact team. We need boundaries in our daily lives and here the group has agreed to share openly, or as much as they choose, and not be in a situation where they then have to be together all the time.

YOUR TURN:

When have you been with a friend or colleague and learned about their deeper life story and been surprised? How did you handle this?

_____
_____
_____
_____

Chapter 17: Impacting Each Other

Just as Kevin was able to handle the distress he could have had about his son stating he was gay, Andrew, the bandana-wearing hairdresser, asked to speak. He was a smooth-talking guy who gave motivational speeches in his industry and he was rarely at a loss for words.

"Vivian," he choked out her name, "Vivian, I cannot thank you enough for this. I have yet to do my SANKOFA Map™ for the group and I was going to leave out some vital information because it is so embarrassing.

"When I went to talk with my mother to get information regarding her childhood, this normally bright and vocal woman resisted talking to me. She is in her fifth marriage and I thought that was the issue … embarrassment because she could not make her relationships work.

"I became really curious and did what was suggested. I took her out to dinner and simply asked for whatever help she could give me to fill in my map. We went back to her apartment after dinner and as we had tea she kept taking deep breaths and finally said, 'Okay, if it will help your business.'

"She then talked about how afraid she was of all the men she married and how she would lock herself in the bedroom rather than be with them."

Talking with our parents in a more open and honest way amazingly can make a difference in how we talk with our bosses, colleagues, and direct reports at work.

"I have learned from this program the power of silence. You all know I am a talker and have, so I thought, most of the answers. So that evening I just sat and used what I learned here and said to my mother, 'Tell me more.'

"It took at least another hour until she finally was able to talk about her uncle who began molesting her when she was ten and told her he would kill her mother if she ever said anything.

"Just those few minutes changed my whole orientation to my childhood and how my mother was always so protective of my two little sisters, and how she would make sure I was never alone with them as we grew up.

"Now it all made sense. Vivian, if you did not have the courage to speak I would have probably kept silent about this. And I also see, since I am in a female-dominated industry and I am a big guy, that I have this residual feeling that no matter what I do I am going to get blamed in the long run. So I have kept to myself with personal dialogue at work, and use the stage and presentations to really let people know who I am. I never let my own personal relationship with women go deeper because sooner or later they will want to keep me at bay."

YOUR TURN:

Think of a time when you learned more about yourself by listening to another person's story. Did you ever tell them, thank them, or just keep it to yourself?

_____

_____

_____

_____

Chapter 18: Complete the Circle

By the time the fourth session came around everyone in the group was freer, lighter, and more connected to the group.

They had all begun to implement the team diversity and inclusion training modules into their work settings and most already sensed employee willingness to see and hear their colleagues in a more balanced and open way.

You now have an understanding of how SANKOFA Mapping™ works and why it is so powerful to do in a group of individuals on a leadership track.

Let's circle back to the beginning with Kathleen from Kumasi, Ghana. T.S. Eliot said it so well:

"We shall not cease from exploration, and the end of all our exploring will be to arrive where we started and know the place for the first time."

Kathleen gave us all an amazing view of growing up in Africa. And her SANKOFA Map™ was, as they all are, filled with universal joys and hurts. For Kathleen, who was 18 when her mother died from cancer, she felt abandoned and insecure. Her father had been with many women, had remarried, and lived in Switzerland working for The World Bank. He had little to do with his daughter, one of three from different relationships, and she felt alone and confused.

Her mother had been a beloved teacher in Kumasi, who was strong-willed when it came to her students and meek when it came to asking anything from this man she had married when still a teen.

Through SANKOFA Mapping™ Kathleen was able to put together a brilliant mosaic of her life and the lives of her ancestors. She saw clearly how women were, and continued to be, second class citizens. Her dream was to help change this.

Her SANKOFA work meant a difficult yet vital conversation with her father whom she barely knew. Gaining courage from her teammates she set up time to have a Skype call with her now, very prosperous and influential father.

Her dialogue centered on his memories of her mother and what it was like to have only daughters. Reporting to the TLC group she said it was the hardest conversation she had ever participated in. And then, with a twinkle, she said she finally began to understand that men were just another sort of human being and her fear of being told she was "NOT" good enough began to untie the "KNOT" in her stomach.

The miracle was her reconnection with her long-deceased mother. She had been angry with her mother for never standing up to her father, or any man in the town. Her mother had been a pleaser and a martyr and Kathleen was, as she said, falling into the same deep pit of pleasing and doing everything for everyone and she hated it.

So what did Kathleen do? She started a scholarship fund at the private school where her mother had taught. She found a reason to stand up and be counted. She was able to go to Accra and begin a campaign for scholarship money for girls who would become future leaders.

What was interesting was that her father became involved and, with his connections, helped his daughter raise money for five girls to go to this prestigious school.

Kathleen was getting strong as she "healed the past to free the present."

And then in the last session where everyone has an opportunity to look at next steps personally and professionally, Kathleen made an announcement.

She was going to run for Parliament. "Yes," she said in a strong voice. "I have the skills and talent; and now that I see myself more whole as a woman and less fearful of men, I am ready."

Eighteen months later, Kathleen was one of very few women in the Parliament of Ghana.

YOUR TURN:

Think of a time you made a powerful change personally and write down the result.

_____
_____
_____
_____

Chapter 19: Putting It All Together

UNIQUE is a powerful way of viewing each other. Different is a way of separating ourselves from others. Will we always "love" one another? Of course not! However, once we can see each other in a new light, often the resentment and anger fade and give way to compassion and appreciation.

Leaders who have done SANKOFA Mapping™ can see in a relatively short time where the "stuck places" are when employees talk with each other. It is always even more obvious when there is conflict to resolve.

Diversity management in conjunction with life stories gives a bold, new way to talk with each other and make positive change happen.

Examples:

• Rose, a teacher, came to Diane the principal who had been through Total Leadership Connections™. Rose said with defiance that it was a racial issue when two other teachers were not cooperating with her. In the course of the discussion Diane asked if there were other places when people did not cooperate. Rose shrugged and mentioned that, "These two remind me of my bitchy sisters. They always ganged up on me and I hated it."

The principal suggested a SANKOFA Coach™ for Rose and quickly Rose was able to see the connection between her upsets with her original organization, the family, and what was going on at work. It was not racial; it was familiar. The principal was then able to help the three teachers work on the school issues with less underlying tension. It took only four coaching sessions for Rose to change her perspective, and the school concerns were handled quickly.

> *A relieved principal stated, "The cost for Rose to have a coach was far less than the cost for the legal issues that were about to explode at school. They would have taken more time and effort and eventually were headed to create a schism in the whole elementary school. It could have gotten really ugly."*

• Ted was the youngest son in a prosperous family business. His father died while he was still a teen and now, in his thirties, he was having difficulty with the new COO who was not a family member yet had the same strong personality as his father. Ted was sure the issues surrounded the fact that the COO was uncomfortable that Ted was gay.

Given a SANKOFA Coach™, Ted was able to get in touch with his underlying fear that his father would never have accepted him. This was the same fear with the COO. Ted was just about ready to leave this family business rather than discuss his concerns. Once he saw the connection he chose to have an honest dialogue with the COO and changes happened quickly and surprisingly easily.

> *"When I went to the COO and started by telling him that my sense of intimidation was from my long ago past and had nothing to do with our present relationship, I got his attention right away. I did not go into detail.*
>
> *"However, just telling him he was not the cause of my upset was, as I have learned, a*

*'pattern interrupt.' He was frustrated with me
because I always held back; and as we talked
we could see that our impasse had less to do
with my being gay and more to do with that
scared fifteen-year-old I had not released.*

*"Not only am I staying with the company I
really love, I now feel free to make a real
contribution and use my creativity fully. Here is
the best part. He wants information on how to
do a SANKOFA Map™. Who knows; I'm sure
he has some dragons to slay in his past life
too."*

• Matthew was the head of a healthcare association. He
was smart and well-respected for his expertise. However,
he had created a mess with his staff because he was
always rescuing the females on his staff and they knew:
"When there is an issue, run to Matthew and he will jump
in and fix it." The males were calling out favoritism.
Matthew just could not see it.

The tensions on the team were underneath the
surface and the toxic environment was becoming an
issue. Matthew initially resisted doing a SANKOFA
Map™ because he felt everything was "just fine"; and
besides, his personal life "had nothing to do with his
work life." Finally the Chair of the Board made the
request and Matthew started to work with a SANKOFA
Coach™ to look at how his past showed up at work.

*"What an eye-opener. When I was twelve
my father committed suicide. I NEVER talked
about it with anyone. However, as I did my
SANKOFA Map™ I was able to see how I was
always there, as I was growing up, to help
everyone, especially my sisters, because I did*

82

not ever want anyone else to be so dejected they would take their own life the way my dad did.

"I now see how destructive that linear thinking can be. This had nothing to do with gender bias, although I can see how it certainly looked like that. I was protecting the women at work so I would not have to look at my internal pain. I am learning to let my staff talk with each other to resolve issues and not jump in to rescue. It is a relief, and more work is getting done more quickly."

Now is the time for you to get a handle on doing your own SANKOFA Map™. Granted doing this in a professional group is the ideal. Contact us for more information about coaches or our next Total Leadership Connections™ (TLC) program. If you do your map alone and hit a snag you can e-mail me at sylvia@ceoptions.com or call us at 570-636-3858 and we will be glad to help.

The next section will give you the outline of how to do your map and also give you an opportunity to look at the 13 most common behavior patterns in the workplace.

You will have an opportunity to look at how someone pushes your buttons and why. This is invaluable information for anyone who leads people or who is on a leadership track.

Keep a pen and paper handy and get ready to take a verbal and visual X-ray of your life and the lives of your ancestors.

Ready? ...... Let's get going!

PART TWO: UNDERSTAND

Universal and Personal Stories
Are Always Connected

"There have been great societies that did not use the wheel, but there have been no societies that did not tell stories." – *Ursula LeGuin*

Now it is time to look at the patterns from the past and how they are being played out in both your personal and professional life. Here you will be given the outline to do your own SANKOFA Map™ or use this while you work with a certified SANKOFA Coach™. The best part is that just about everyone who has ever used our model comes away with a sense of amazement saying, "I have more energy. I am seeing with clearer lenses." What we have seen is freedom to have deeper, more authentic dialogue both at work, home, and in the community.

Chapter 20: The Never-Ending Story

You now have a view of the power of story, someone else's story. From Shakespeare to Spielberg we know that story captivates, engages and helps us understand the meaning of life.

There is no culture that does not include story. Way back when, before the written word, oral tradition was used to share history, customs, rituals and legends. Why does story have so much power? Because it connects us with one another; it is like salve on the aches and pains of long journeys; it makes us feel less alone.

In the past, powerful tales were usually told by the tribal elders to the younger generations. These stories were used to teach about love, leadership, and honor.

Your gift, your SANKOFA Map™, can live on for generations to come – a legacy of leadership.

Now is the time for you to join the ranks of the storytellers throughout history; your ancestors are waiting, the world is waiting.

Take a deep breath. You are about to come face-to-face with your greatness, with the twists and turns that make you UNIQUE.

Here are the rules for doing your SANKOFA Map™. Nothing is off-limits. Nothing is too small to be ignored. Everything is significant; everything!

You will begin to redefine the meaning of memory, truth, trust, hope, despair, courage, determination, deceit, depression, and forgiveness.

**The freedom that comes
from knowing what has helped
to form you gives you power
over the choices you make
moving forward.**

Sylvia Lafair, PhD

You will begin to see the patterns that connect, the way a system whirls and swirls. You will see that in one generation there may have been stagnation, and in another constant growth. In one generation there may have been war and suffering; several generations later, great wealth and perhaps even a worship of money.

You find where you fit and how the patterns that connect have put their mark on you. And then you get to decide. Yes, you get to decide which outdated patterns have been like chains around your ankles and which are so brilliant you want to polish them and keep them stage front at all times.

What if ... you had in your lineage those who stood for what is right and decent and it cost them their lives? You can begin to see how that has impacted you. Have you and your family continued to speak out or stay silent?

What if ... you had in your family someone who murdered his spouse and then killed himself? (A woman in our TLC program had to grapple with being the daughter this exact scenario.) Do you keep away from relationships and live a life of abject fear, or look at the situation from the eyes of compassion? Have you looked for an unstable partner, or do you look for someone who is a kind and gentle human?

What if ... you have a history of slavery, holo-caust, royalty, poverty, mental illness, or mental greatness? How do you take all of this and connect the dots for your own life, right here, right now, at home and at work?

An important message as you do your map that will be told again and again: telling the truth is NOT spilling your guts. You are in charge of how much or how little you tell in any given situation. "Do not throw pearls before swine" is an old quotation. Do not share deeply to be made fun of or ignored.

As you do your SANKOFA Map™ you will hone your intuition and learn when is the right time to talk or to be quiet.

There are two parts to the SANKOFA Map™. One is to see where you fit in the larger, vaster landscape of life. You will begin to connect the dots between the "begot and the begotten."

This is more than just a history of who became a parent and who was there to care and help, and who was there to hinder. All fit and come together to make YOU be YOU.

The second part of doing the SANKOFA Map™ is to learn about YOU in the workplace, in the here and now; who and what pushes your buttons, and what you want to do about it. It is about YOU as a leader.

Once you can see clearly how family, culture, and crises became the braided ropes to your reactions, you can see which of the 13 patterns are "sticky," the ones with your name on them. You can see how being the "rebel" or "super-achiever" or "clown" was part of your destiny until now and you can make change happen.

You are on the road to positive and powerful leadership. You are ready to make your brilliant contribution in your own UNIQUE way, as only you can; ready to look the patterns in the eye and tell them YOU are in charge NOW!

Chapter 21: Invisible Loyalties Released

"Why are these patterns so powerful and who really cares?" you shrug. They hold incessant power because they are invisible. You cannot throw a rock at them; you cannot stamp them to the ground.

They lock in, often for generations (as you will soon see), and cause you to respond in knee-jerk ways. Often they make you do things before you are ready to respond.

Take some time and watch Steven Spielberg's trilogy *Back to the Future.* Be patient, it will take until the third film to see how stopping a knee-jerk pattern can save lives.

Brilliant work, Spielberg!!!!

Patterns are there initially as protection devices. They helped keep your ancestors safe or your ancestors made adjustments to the system to go from unsafe to safe. You see, way deep down we are programmed to survive as best we can for the survival of the species.

What worked when you were a kid may be outdated now. What may have worked when your ancestors were tilling the soil may not be practical now.

You cannot initially see your own annoying invisible patterns; it's always easier to see what is wrong with someone else.

SANKOFA first gives you the opportunity to OBSERVE. Then you move quickly to UNDERSTAND. Once you identify which patterns define your behavior you begin to understand how they arose; and soon you can take specific actions to transform them to their healthy and positive opposites.

Take the long view for your personal life as you zero in to find the hidden patterns of habitual office behavior that make you less effective than you would like to be in your work setting.

This is also the time for you to really get a handle on where you are still stuck with the darn prejudices that are the tainted stains of judging by becoming Pattern-Aware™.

Chapter 22: Patterns Interrupted

Just before you take out pen and paper to do your map look at the following list of patterns. These 13 are the most common patterns in the workplace that I have put together after decades of coaching executives and teams. There are more; however these 13 are certainly enough to work with. They are the same in every type of organization, and show up globally in all cultures.

We can all make a case for succumbing to one or another pattern from time to time. However, there are often two or three that "have our name on them."

For me I had to own drama queen, pleaser, rebel and, from time to time (one I hated to admit to), victim. Yup, I can do a mighty good victim in the right circumstances; Academy Award material.

This is another form of diversity management; to see that we all have fallen into patterns from family and culture, which are not as obvious as race, gender and the like that often cause us to turn away from each other.

Here is the list. See which ones call to you. Even better, stop reading and go to www.sylvia lafair.com/pattern-aware-quiz and take the Pattern-Aware™ Quiz. It has been proven to be eye-opening and makes some people upset, while others get a hearty laugh and say, "Wow that nailed me!"

One senior executive called our office, stunningly upset. He complained that his results showed he was an avoider and he insisted that was just not the case.

When asked, "How long ago did you take the quiz?" he responded, "Two months ago. I was just not ready to discuss it back then." BINGO.

Here are the patterns:

Super-achiever – must win at all costs.
Rebel – can't accept any authority.
Procrastinator – won't finish anything.
Clown – reduces everything to a joke.
Persecutor – bullies people into misery.
Victim – too scared to take any action.
Rescuer – must be the hero who saves others.
Drama Queen/King – makes emotional scenes.
Martyr – does everyone else's work.
Pleaser – says what folks want to hear.
Avoider – dodges work and responsibility.
Denier – pretends problems do not exist.
Splitter – secretly sets up conflict.

What is fascinating with these patterns is how easy it is to see your boss as the super-achiever, your co-worker as the rescuer, your sister as the martyr, and your mother-in-law as the splitter. It is harder to look at yourself; and yet, to make real progress it is vital to be true to that little voice inside that says, "Pay attention; you really do behave that way!"

Chapter 23: Digging Deep and Fast

Remember the stories from Total Leadership Connections™? Kathleen, our African butterfly, saw clearly that the pleaser pattern had her name on it. Mike, the transgender doctor, was clearly a rebel; and Andrew, the salon owner, saw that being a super-achiever had a downside.

Now it is your turn.

By doing the SANKOFA Map™ you can begin the process of understanding and eventually healing the hurts from the past, and continue to build upon the patterns that reinforce such virtues as respect, courage, tenacity, and altruism. You can admit where you have fallen victim or been a persecutor or denied the reality of what has been happening, or run to hide and not stand strong.

In essence, what you want to do – what this book will help you do – is harness and eventually transform the critical patterns that can help you achieve optimal success at home and at work.

We are all needed to break down the walls of prejudice and the ugly words that discount those with whom we share this home called Earth.

By seeing the patterns clearly you have the opportunity to literally flip them over to their healthy, positive opposites.

It is so important to know that you will not be left with a negative behavior pattern that you cannot change and then have to walk around with it tattooed on your forehead.

No, the good news is with a bit of strength training, the pattern is waiting to be changed. However, this is not a quick fix like a pill to swallow. You have to become vigilant to observe, understand … and then stop, breath and take charge to transform.

You can do it!

Hundreds have used this model to change their lives and to change the direction of diversity management and leadership development in many, many organizations.

Changing behavior in anything beyond a superficial way requires discipline, time, and commitment. When you pay attention to the patterns while you do your SANKOFA Map™ the rewards are amazing. You will find more honest communication, better relationships, optimized teamwork, better financial results and, of course, the deep fulfillment that comes with living a more authentic life.

Chapter 24: Breaking Free

Now, let's get to the SANKOFA Map™.

A SANKOFA Map™ is a very expressive, personal statement. It is like a sketch or a letter written by hand.

Why start with family? There is nowhere else to start!

A family is a weaving of multiple colors and textures. There is ancestry filled with joy, pain, fear, courage, betrayal, kindness, and connectedness.

Each generation hosts a new set of individuals and each individual takes the ancient stories and remakes them into something meaningful to him or her.

We are the link from the past to the future. Our task is not to repeat the patterns that have come before us; our task is to stand on the shoulders of our history and our relations.

While families dream of homeostasis, always yearning to stay the same, the same forever and ever, this is not what nature intended. Our job is to grow. To grow is to repair, to build upon. To grow is to learn about the fragility and limitations of our parents, grandparents, and great-grandparents.

To grow is to understand our vulnerability and their vulnerability, and develop strength where there was none before. Our task is to move forward, to untie the binds of the past, to create relationships that are meaningful and sustainable and help support us on our journey.

There is only one ticket to get to this planet and it comes from the two people who formed us.

The family is the most basic, the most intense, and the most powerful system in the world. The only ticket to get to this planet is through the two people who constitute our initial family. We may call them Mom and Dad; we may call them "identity unknown"; we may prefer one or the other.

What we cannot do regarding our original family is "ex" them out. There is no such thing as an "ex-mother" or an "ex-father." Only by first accepting and observing the past, then understanding it, and finally transforming it is there freedom to choose our behavior as adults and reach our true potential personally and professionally.

What we cannot do is "X" them out. They cannot, nor will not, go away. Our first feelings center on them and how they welcomed us into the world. We can cater to them, ignore them, rebel against them, run away from them, or enjoy them.

This includes adoption and foster care. It includes test tube babies. While these situations are certainly more complex we still need to consider the power of the source and make decisions on whether we want to or have the right to seek out our birth parents. Doing the map will help you understand and decide what to do if there are gaps in your chart.

This is why we create our SANKOFA Map™. To get a grander view of what came before us, our parents, our siblings, and to explore what happened generation upon generation ago that has now tumbled right into our laps as part of our legacy.

Next we look at the patterns and tendencies that help determine our behavior at work. I want to help you consider the gifts and challenges that have been handed through the generations. In every family, in every life, there are positive moments as well as struggling, suffering, and conflict.

It is the complex whole that makes us who we are. I want to help you become not only more observant and less reactive to the anxiety and stress life offers but also more attuned to the strengths in even the most difficult family environment.

Chapter 25: Becoming a Map Builder

The SANKOFA Map™ is like an electrical chart. It is comprised of circles and squares. The circles represent the female lineage and the squares are the males. It is interesting that in most cultures the circle stands for wholeness, for continuity (whether females have children or not, this gender represents that continuity). Squares with four sides represent solidity and safety. This has been the symbol chosen for the male gender and goes back to tribal times where men were the providers of the safe place for the women to raise the children.

Start at the middle of a piece of paper. Begin by putting the circle for your mother and the square for your father. Underneath the symbols, put their dates of birth and dates of death if needed. An X through the circle or square serves as a quick visual representation of the deaths in your family. Now add their siblings (your aunts and uncles) with as much information as you have.

You can also make notes on a separate piece of paper to be ready for your presentation. If your parents are still alive you want to go for the gold; set some time to ask them questions about their own memories of their parents, brothers, and sisters.

Go back as far as you can. The Internet is an amazing source of information and many who have done the SANKOFA Map™ have found relatives as well as information that has been powerful and at times even life-changing.

Here is what a map looks like, ready to fill in the names and dates of birth, death, and other milestones. Note that it's a vertical view of the horizontal chart.

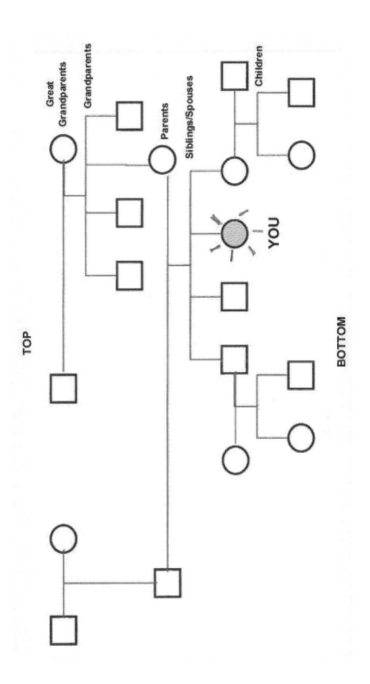

Once you have put the map on paper there are important questions to ponder; and if possible, ask the members of your family to help you fill in the blanks.

HEALTH: Look for patterns of specific illnesses, sudden deaths, addictions, suicides, etc. Look for who did the caretaking and who chose to let others do all the heavy lifting of caretaking. Were people willing to explore new options for health concerns, or did they rely on the traditional medical profession? What were the said and unsaid messages about health, about habits of smoking, exercise, eating well?

WEALTH: Look at the role of money in your family. Was money spent on vacations or only on specific needs? Was it a "saving" environment or one of excessive spending? Did gambling play into the family dynamics? Was money talked about or was it kept a secret? Was money given to charity or only used for personal wants and needs?

RELATIONSHIPS: Is there a pattern of overly-close family ties (enmeshment) or lots of distance between family members (disengaged)? Are conversations kept superficial to not "rock the boat" or can they go deep into how people really feel? Were there favorites and those who were ignored or talked about in a negative way most of the time? Were there family secrets and lots of collusion about "don't tell"? How are youngsters encouraged or discouraged from following their dreams?

WORK: What is the pattern of success or failure in the family? Is work seen as creative and fun or as drudgery to just get the paycheck? What do people in the family do to gain attention from their work? Who were the leaders in the family to explore uncharted new work territory? Was there a message to play it safe, or play full out at work?

SPIRITUALITY: How important was religious practice or affiliation? How do religious beliefs impact marriage, parenting, sexuality, and family responsibilities? What happens to those who have opposing points of view? Is there room for discussion about religion or is it meant to be put under wraps? How has the family belief about spirituality been affected by the larger cultural environment?

Chapter 26: Discovery is the Platinum Card

The purpose of SANKOFA goes way beyond an interesting chart to discuss when there is a lull in a conversation. It is the tool for discovering important connections between elements of your family background and your own personal day-to-day present patterns.

Here are some things to please take into consideration. Every family is both functional and dysfunctional. Doing the map is an exercise in compassion. It is a way to see diversity from the human dimension rather than as a series of statistics and charts.

There are courageous individuals and cowards in all families. Your task is to see the long view, as much as possible, and how the variety of cultures played a role in how people behaved. Each generation was given a set of patterns on how to behave, what was safe and what was out of bounds. Like a set of good dishes they got passed from generation to generation.

Looking from a cultural perspective you can see how the different norms of the times dictated how men and women behaved, how racial injustices occurred, how religion often cast a spell, who stood up and who spoke out and who remained silent.

You also can see the role that crises played. Be it war or natural disaster, or a sudden death by illness or car or plane crash, these crises result in what I call "hardening of the emotions."

When a crisis occurs, the impact can last for many generations unless it is surfaced and discussed and the fear, anger, contempt, depression, and other emotions are laid to rest with the moments of pain and hurt.

This is not about wishing people were different, not about railing against unfair fates. It is about seeing how YOU have been impacted by events often from long ago and deciding what to do about it.

Once you understand
your lineage, you can decide
what to transform.

A word about secrets; they are the proverbial skeletons locked away in dark, dusty closets.

Think about Vivian who kept her secret of sexual abuse from her children, even after they were grown. It was not until she sat with her son and daughter and told them what happened that they began to soften their perspective toward a mother they loved but could never really get close to. And they both began to understand why Vivian was overprotective toward her daughter and kept her at arm's length from her son.

You will, like Ruth was able to do, see your parents beyond a one-dimensional perspective. You will see your parents as lively, pulsating beings who were boundless children and tempestuous teenagers, not just those big people who bossed you around or who were never there for you ... from your own child eyes.

You will see how cultures that want sameness and stigmatize anyone who is unique and different cause so much pain and undercurrents of despair, as we can see when Nazi Germany only wanted a special super-race of blond, blue-eyed humans, and the lengths they went to in that deadly experiment.

SANKOFA Mapping™ and becoming Pattern-Aware™ will help you untie the "NOTS" that have hardened as "KNOTS" of fear, retribution, and angst.

As you will find, studying your SANKOFA Map™ will move you beyond a one-dimensional perspective of parent-child relationships. No longer will the more simple "I liked my mother better" or "my father was an absent parent" will suffice. You will begin to see these people with their own struggles, their own hopes and dreams, and you will get a clear look at how your parents passed on to you their ways of relating.

It is an eye-opening experience. It helps you become, at any age, a more grown-up version of yourself.

Now you are getting ready for the most enticing part of the diversity management journey. As a leader you are getting ready to TRANSFORM your organization to one of purposeful collaboration and success.

Once you have your whole story mapped out you can begin to pick and choose the stories you want to tell at work. This is where there is so much power. You can take time to write down bits and pieces of what you want to say in a meeting, of what is appropriate to a colleague, of how to help someone when you give a performance review.

Chapter 27: Let Me Tell You a Story

Why are stories so powerful? And even more important, why is your story vital as a leadership strategy?

First, let me ask you a question. "How much does a PowerPoint presentation fire you up to really go out there and make change happen, or get your team to do better, or risk having a straight conversation with your boss?"

I have asked this to thousands of people and what I get back is a bemused smile, and maybe a verbal response of "You have got to be kidding."

We all have, as you already see, a profound need to grasp the patterns of living. The human mind has an urge to make order out of chaos, to define patterns. We have a need to understand patterns. We love to look at the symmetry of a pinecone, the stripes of a zebra, and the rings around Saturn.

There is pattern and order in the universe. We have to learn to read it. There are patterns in our own DNA. Our task is to seek understanding of the interconnectedness of all life and become more astute to see form and pattern everywhere.

What better place to discover and dissect pattern than in the universal stories we all share? As Joseph Campbell would suggest, we are all on a hero's journey.

Using story at work is becoming more and more requested. This is the added benefit you get from doing your SANKOFA Map™.

Stories express how and why life changes, and how to deal with the forces of fear and risk and difficult decisions.

UNIQUE: How Story Sparks Diversity, Inclusion, and Engagement

Once you do your SANKOFA Map™ you learn to unite an idea with an emotion so you can tell a compelling story. You want to harness the imagination of your listeners and ask them to join you in a new way of working together.

What better place than with leadership, diversity, and inclusion?

Neuro-economist Paul Zak's research indicates that while listening to the tense moments in a story our brains produce the stress hormone cortisol, which allows us to focus. When something of a positive nature happens in the story we release oxytocin, the feel-good chemical that promotes empathy and caring. And when there is a happy ending to a story the brain triggers the limbic system, the brain's reward center, to release dopamine, which makes us feel hopeful and optimistic.

Here is an example from my SANKOFA Map™, my story about how I have become so passionate developing leaders who are not afraid to speak out and handle conflict effectively and see the power of diversity and inclusion.

Notice how there are tension, positive moments, and a happy ending that is geared toward moving the listener toward a better vision for the future.

Watching my father die from a heart attack when I was fourteen lit a fire under my ass to live a life of outrageous adventure.

I climbed the Great Pyramid in Giza, hiked the Inca Trail into Machu Picchu, meditated with monks at the Shaolin Temple in China, and ate indiscernible stew in the Amazon with a Shaman.

All of this was, in part, to run away from my grief, and cover over the anger I felt with my father and two of his brothers who had a lucrative family business that was fiscally sound but emotionally bankrupt.

In my grief I saw clearly that they could never resolve conflict. It was just competing and fighting. They never saw each other in a positive light.

When I asked why they were always bickering, I would hear, "We are just so different from each other." And the stress finally got to my dad.

Different, that word was a killer.

So rather than climb mountains I decided to look for the "cure" for different.

How many others have had lives destroyed because of that word?

My life, my passion, is about leadership and transformation, about offering the most effective tools for the human side of business. And I ask all leaders to join me so we can all put "different" aside and let UNIQUE blossom.

That is my story.

I know yours is equally important. Now that you have unearthed your life story via your SANKOFA Map™ you are ready for the major reason to be here, right here, right now: to change what no longer works, to take your place at the leadership table, and share your successes with the world.

Storytelling is powerful. Life happens in story form. Stories go where no statistics can go. Stories can embed data; however, it will not inspire people to act. Stories, your story, can fire your staff's imagination and touch their hearts.

All of the work you have done until now hinges on taking your story into the world and transforming it in your own UNIQUE way.

UNIQUE: How Story Sparks Diversity,
Inclusion, and Engagement

Get ready for Part Three.
No hesitation.
Let's get going.

PART THREE: TRANSFORM

We Are All in It Together

"When we quit thinking primarily about ourselves and our own self-preservation, we undergo a truly heroic transformation of consciousness." – *Joseph Campbell*

You now have the opportunity to become a pioneer in the world of UNIQUE, going way past "different." There are programs you can take into your work setting and make diversity management shine as the foundation on which all work stands. There will be more collaboration, more creative input, more camaraderie, and more organizational health. This section will give ideas for creating your own programs or using some of those I have developed over the years.

Chapter 28: Caterpillars into Butterflies

Remember Phillip, the pharmaceutical VP who introduced me to the film *Sankofa*? Back then he said with such bitterness that America had a "great tag line" and that "land of the free and home of the brave" was just so much branding bullshit.

Phillip eventually went through the Total Leadership Connections™ program and did his SANKOFA Map™. He reluctantly peeled the layers back to finally see the roots of his anger and despair. Until that time he was sadly embarrassed and ashamed of his family.

He was the first to ever go to college and he saw his relatives as lazy procrastinators. They had menial jobs and would rather go to the local bar after work than better themselves; or so he thought.

A business trip took him within thirty miles of his cousins in Alabama; and with cheerleading from his TLC class he went to talk with them. The SANKOFA search led him to a rickety old frame house that needed paint. He sat sipping tea with his factory-working relatives and said more than once, "Wow, I never knew that before."

One of the "I never knew" elements was that his great-grandfather had gone to jail for slugging a white man who hit a little Negro child who was late with a grocery delivery. Philip had never asked and merely assumed that Great-Granddaddy was in jail for drunkenness so common in his family.

In his own words, "SANKOFA Mapping™ gave me a totally new perspective of my family. Suddenly I have a sense of pride that someone stood up to that bigoted bully. I also see that my super-achiever pat-tern was to make up for all the dead wood in the family."

This very talented man could now begin the journey from overstressed and dogmatic super-achiever to creative collaborator and work more productively with his team.

Recently receiving a promotion to COO of his company he wrote, "My new job would never have come about if I had not gone to sit on that old wood porch in Alabama. I really did 'heal the past to free the present.' And I shared the highlights of my story with the executive leadership team at an off-site. Just what you predicted happened. Others began to share and soon we were more open and more connected than I ever thought possible. Thanks."

TRANSFORMATION AT WORK includes using SANKOFA stories that have a take-away message and will linger with the audience.

In many companies, SANKOFA Mapping™ is now part of individual development plans. This is a way for leaders in a one-to-one setting to come face-to-face with their patterns and find new, positive ways to be effective. Learning about life patterns and how they impact at work is invaluable. Taking this information and finding just the right stories at the right time is a leadership art and craft widely required these days.

Diversity and inclusion then becomes part of team building, part of town hall meetings, part of strategic planning meetings, and even part of one-to-one casual coffee meet-ups.

We need to break the old pattern that says logic and statistics are more professional. Not so!

If you stick with facts and numbers and worry that storytelling is too emotional and even manipulative (who says statistics don't manipulate?) you are missing the point. Emotions work better because they reach both minds and hearts. The staff gets to see the real you and that is what they want. It is what we all want – honesty and openness.

Leaders who are in touch with their patterns talk to their teams differently. It is not necessary to do what Phillip did and share part of a story. Often it is just enough to help a team understand that you, the leader, have been transforming your own mindset and you are working on changing what has not helped in the past.

Arthur is a great example. His team was frustrated because whenever there was a conflict and they went to him to bring up tense issues he would immediately send them to Human Resources. They wanted his guidance and it was simply out of reach.

Until, doing several personal sessions with a SANKOFA Coach™, he was able to see where he was stuck. It was just under the radar, an itch he could not until now scratch to get relief.

Arthur was of Asian origin and yet, since he had come to the U.S. at age seven, he felt he was totally "Americanized."

Not so.

In doing his SANKOFA Map™ he realized he was an avoider, a theme that ran throughout his family and throughout much of his culture. He was taught not to argue, that conflicts were to be avoided at any cost.

That was all he shared with his team at an off-site. He then committed to turning things around and that he was working on the positive opposite of the avoider, the initiator. While it was uncomfortable, he was willing to be the initiating force to discuss situations that were tense and stay with it until they were solved.

Arthur is now stronger in his understanding of the patterns in his life and is able to ask his team to come directly to him. And if he starts to "fall down the mountain" back to old habits, he requests they give him a gentle nudge.

In a group or individually, SANKOFA Mapping™ rocks!

Chapter 29: Appetizers for the Team

Another way of offering diversity and inclusion training based on the principles outlined here is to help intact teams begin to see how the 13 most common patterns in the workplace collide with each other at work and what to do about it.

Think of it this way: sometimes the bumps on your head fit the holes in someone else's head!

Often employees will claim gender bias or cultural inequities, or the like, when really it is those darn patterns at play. Once we can get at observation about the patterns and what it takes to transform them, conflict is handled faster and smarter.

For example, often an avoider and a drama queen will get into it. The more noise the drama queen makes the faster the avoider runs away. It becomes an unconscious game. Noise-run, noise-run, noise-run!

Of course they both want resolution to the situation. However, they are so "pattern-skilled" that the drama queen thinks, "If only I say it again and louder he will hear me." and the avoider thinks, "If only I get away she will learn to be less demanding." They are stuck in a vortex of conditioning and it wastes time.

**Until we transform patterns
we are at their mercy, and
productivity and creativity
are diminished.**

While this may have some underpinnings of gender or race issues, they can now be seen through the lens of pattern transformation. What I mean is that most conflict situations are much easier to resolve when looked at as ingrained, old, time-wasting patterns and how they can absolutely be transformed to their positive opposites.

Giving people an action plan and ways to talk with each other more effectively, to have PEP Talks™ about the issue at hand and acknowledging one's own behavior, is very freeing. As we have seen, most of our unconscious biases were learned before we could even read. Learning to observe them and understand them makes transforming them by becoming PatternAware™ a clear action method with profound results.

Think about Cynthia and Tom for a minute. Cynthia reports to Tom. They are part of a high level sales team. They are both of Chinese origin. Cynthia, a pleaser, is furious with Tom for being a persecutor. She says he micromanages and is never content with her work.

They had a meeting to air out their differences and find an action plan to continue to work together effectively. What came out in this facilitated session is that Cynthia had lots of frustration with "bossy men" yet would always say "yes" to whatever was asked. Tom fit the category perfectly.

As they talked they saw the patterns clearly and the cultural implications as well. In their culture women were taught to please and men to dominate. Living in America (both were born on mainland China) the norms have changed, yet the patterns deep inside have remained the same.

They looked at the pattern transformation list (hold on, it is there for you in a few pages) and agreed to work together in a new way. Tom, as a persecutor turned visionary, was willing to see Cynthia, in fact all women, in a more equal way and Cynthia was willing to be a truth-teller and not hold back due to her old conditioning.

It took time and adjustments. The good news is that they were willing to make the changes. They were both able to see and also hear the way they looked and sounded to each other. They learned to respect each other in a new light and the end result was higher productivity.

Here is one more example ... The Tragic Triangle:

When a persecutor (aka bully) is upset, she will find a victim to berate. The victim puts his head down and says, "Yes it is entirely my fault; it is always my fault; just keep the judging, blaming, and attacking coming my way. I deserve it." Now, here is the most important part. When these two get into it, suddenly, like magic, the rescuer appears.

Question: Who does the rescuer rescue? Why the victim, of course.

The rescuer will always finish the victim's work or take on the persecutor and tell her why she is wrong and defend the victim. This tragic triangle keeps people in their roles and again is a time and efficiency waster. It is certainly toxic and everyone else just sits around and watches. It is really like a very bad sitcom. We all know there has to be a better way.

Now we are ready to take the OUT Technique™ to a new level.

What happens at work when we begin to take action to deal with our patterns and help each other deal with theirs?

Once you can have a whole team observe their patterns and then (and this is really the most important part) see that they can be transformed to ways of relating that are more positive and more effective ... wow! Then you have a team of "unbeatables."

As one person in a system (a team) begins to change, there are opportunities for profound changes in others to open up.

Now that the 13 most common patterns that get in the way in the workplace have been identified, we are ready to look at what happens when these patterns are transformed.

This can be done by using what I have named PEP Talk™ which stands for Pattern Encounter Process.

PEP Talks™ can be used in conjunction with the 13 patterns and just about everyone I have worked with has found the patterns and the pattern transformation work to be equally fun and challenging.

If you are a leader and want a team of unique "unbeatables," give them the tools of the PEP Talk™ and let this be a way of working together that is both eye-opening and invigorating.

Initially you can take a team through this exercise in a two-hour program to get a handle on the patterns as follows:

Have the team take the PatternAware™ Quiz (www.sylvialafair.com) and begin to look at the situations where stress causes us to revert back to outdated, ingrained patterns from childhood for security and survival.

Let the team talk about "what presses their buttons" and what they normally do when someone is particularly annoying. This is usually a high-energy, interactive time of "OBSERVING" what happens when we respond without really taking a breath or thinking though the implications of our behavior.

"A great many people think they are thinking when they are merely rearranging prejudices." – William James

Now for the BIG benefit of learning about patterns, pattern transformation. The Chinese have a saying: "The bigger the front, the bigger the back." I am sure you are wondering, as I did, "What the heck does that mean?"

It means we already have everything within us – the good and the bad, the sublime and the ridiculous. The more potential for bad we have, the more potential for good is also there. We can see when someone wants to change their behavior and become a beacon of light, they can do that, even from a prison cell.

What we are doing when we transform our patterns is taking all the energy in one way of behaving and turning it upside down to its healthier, more productive opposite.

For example, when someone has used their energy to avoid difficult situations they can flip this to become initiators and start the conversation for change rather than run from it. Someone who was programmed to be a rebel and would run to H.R. or to a lawyer with a grievance can become a community builder to help change the system from the inside out.

I personally have worked to change my drama queen hissy fits to get attention to become a good storyteller and use that need for drama in a more effective way.

This is what you want to help your team strive for, to observe, understand, and then finally trans-form the patterns that no longer work to the ones that are positive and effective.

Here is the list of the pattern transformations, and then we will give some direction on how to do the PEP Talk.

- Super-Achiever – must win at all costs; Transforms to Creative Collaborator who sees the importance of teamwork and knows no one wins unless we all do

- Rebel – can't accept authority; Transforms to Community Builder who pulls people together for positive change and impacts the larger group

- Procrastinator – won't finish anything; Transforms to Realizer who has a sense that all things are possible

- Clown – reduces everything to a joke; Transforms to Humorist who uses humor at the right moments; timing is everything

- Persecutor – bullies people into misery; Transforms to Visionary who practices the art and craft of conflict transformation and sees the big picture

- Victim – too scared to take any action; Transforms to Explorer who is curious and adven-turous, finding new ways to solve problems

- Rescuer – demands to be the big hero; Transforms to Mentor who listens and gives good advice at the right time

- Drama Queen/King – makes emotional scenes; Transforms to Storyteller who unites those around them to collaborate by using good stories for motivation

- Martyr – does everyone else's work; Transforms to Integrator who brings people together to share the work load so no one feels over-burdened

- Pleaser – says what folks want to hear; Transforms to Truth Teller who can tell the truth without grand-standing or lecturing

- Avoider – runs away when confronted; Transforms to Initiator who steps up to handle conflict and no longer fears being judged

- Denier – pretends problems don't exist; Transforms to Trust Builder who faces all problems directly and asks lots of questions

- Splitter – secretly sets up conflict; Transforms to Peacemaker who works to preserve the integrity of the whole system, not one person or one team over another

As you learn to incorporate these pattern transformations into office PEP Talks™ remember that these more desirable patterns of behavior are not new patterns, but merely the old ones turned into a happier direction – caterpillars flying away as resplendent butter-flies.

Chapter 30: Cheerleaders and PEP Talks

It is NOT enough to identify and understand your patterns. You also have to commit to push beyond your comfort zone and take positive actions.

You can say, "Yup, that's me," and close the book. You can say. "Yup, that's me and that is where I learned to play it safe." However, without moving to the level of INTERACTION, nothing will really change. All of this will have been a waste of time. Better, you can say "Yup, that's me and I want to make change happen."

ACTION is the key.
And INTERACTION is even
more to the point.

Change comes about when we interact with our bosses, colleagues, and direct reports. We cannot just think about saying something "someday" we need to gain the courage to move to dialogue to insure there will be higher productivity and creative endeavors at work.

As we talk and listen, and respond and listen, and reframe what we say and listen, and acknowledge and listen, the "NOTS" and the "KNOTS" of our lives come loose. We are freer and have more options for how to be authentic in this world of ours.

Here is a thought to ponder: transformation is continuously transforming. What you wish for changes as you grow. To become a leader you must become comfortable on the confusing, exciting, rocky road that never ends. And that is where so many leaders fall down. They do not know how to stay straight and steady with constant change.

There is always a window of opportunity for transformation to occur. Many choose (unconsciously) the path of illness. Others have to work through broken relationships; and still others walk the path of failed jobs to wake them up. Some meet an "important stranger" who will divert them from their path. Money, sex, adoration, alcohol, and drugs are there to lure us away from becoming the best we can be.

At some point we all must go into the woods to face our fears and the dread that we will never come out. In most fairytales and myths, designed to show us the path of transformation, the hero or heroine must touch the deeper unconscious part of themselves to become stronger and more capable to lead.

Here in the woods we engage in battle; wrestle; come to see, know, and ultimately integrate the parts of ourselves we have not wanted to see or been capable of knowing. We must dive into the depths of ourselves in order to be free. This is the ultimate meaning of being authentic.

When you do your PEP Talk™ you are, in a sense, in a battle with yourself. Just about everyone who does this process thinks it is a piece of cake, especially when they watch others. It is always so easy to start by telling another about their patterns and the things they must change. It is a whole different story when we are there to talk about our own personal weaknesses and things that we personally must change.

As you begin the PEP Talk™, keep in mind that this is for your transformation, for you to become a stronger, more adept leader. Ready....

Here is the PEP Talk™ model:

You begin a PEP Talk™ with another by deciding who is still pushing your buttons and who you really need to have a conversation with. It is a good idea to practice this beforehand with a friend or your SANKOFA Coach™.

You can ask someone to take the role of the person who is super-annoying to you.

You play yourself.

Give your helper a full description of the other, including the person's physical characteristics, the person's job responsibilities, how the person communicates, and how the person tends to react emotionally.

As you role-play the scene, please, please remember this is your opportunity to be a leader, and model the power of what happens when YOU are accountable for YOUR behavior. It is THEN that others are more willing to change and meet you in that field beyond right and wrong.

Everyone who has ever done a PEP Talk™ in our Total Leadership Connections™ program has been amazed at how easy it is to listen to and coach others, and how difficult it is once on the "hot seat" to be clear and stay open.

**When you fall into the
judgment trap you are already
prepared for a fight that will
have an ugly ending.**

The natural tendency is to talk about the other person and their patterns, how we want the other person to change, and what upsets us about them. It is so much easier and comforting rather than focusing on and taking responsibility for ourselves.

Here are some examples. How you begin the PEP Talk™ is always the most important part. This is the final product after at least six to ten attempts to say it right:

- "I tend to be very confrontational and push my perspective to get my way. This has been a sure way to shut you down. I value what you have to say and want us to talk with each other in a more effective way. I really need your input about the new sales manager and who you think should train him." (persecutor to visionary)

- "Thanks for meeting with me. I must admit I was hoping that our teams could work this out themselves. However, now that I see I was avoiding this discussion it is not fair to any of us. I want to get your ideas and also offer some suggestions on how to move out of this impasse." (avoider to initiator)

- "I was so bent on keeping you in your present job I did not pay attention to the fact that you are growing at warp speed. It hit me like a ton of bricks that you are really ready for a promotion and I want us to look at options so you will stay with this company and I can support the next move." (denier to trust builder)

- "I get so upset when I think I did not do a good job that I just shut down and don't talk. I want to explore how I can come to discuss a failed project with you next time it happens. Just telling you this is a step. I promise to have at least three new ideas on what can be done differently." (victim to explorer)

- "The last time we were in a meeting I told some really dumb jokes to keep the stress level down. I now look back and see that all I did was deflect the important issues at hand. I will be more vigilant with my humor and I request that if the stress hits me again in the *funny bone* please feel free to stop me." (clown to humorist)

Why bother to admit your deficits to another? Won't that make you weak and put you in the loser position?

This is absolutely not how we have been trained to behave.

Agreed.

However, that model at work is not working. The number of individuals who are unhappy at work is astounding. The number of complaints to Human Resources and to lawyers is astronomical. Perhaps a more human way of talking and being is needed now more than ever.

Chapter 31: Mixing It Up

There have been vast numbers of studies that all show companies with gender, race, and cultural diversity have higher productivity and better organizational cultures.

Mixing it up stimulates creativity.

When there is diversity in all of its messy and chaotic forms, it is alive and juicy. And, we need to learn to handle messy. It is where the business edge is in this century. Conformity often leads to mediocre decisions and limited creative input.

Group think, that type of behavior where everyone just goes along, everyone nods and agrees, turns into lack of discussion among individuals. Sooner or later we become bored and rote. Conversations become a game of masquerade. And even bigger, there is lack of creative input.

As we learn to know ourselves through our SANKOFA Maps™ and becoming PatternAware™ we are able to handle the richness of those who come into our worlds. We are no longer fearful of speaking up. We value dissention yet see the opportunities for connection. We are safe to tell our stories in their simplest and most credible, concrete and emotional form. We listen differently.

**Companies that encourage
life-long learning and offer
opportunities for self-awareness
programs have an edge in
retaining the best and
the brightest.**

Will companies prosper who encourage their leaders and employees to know themselves? Is this a "fluffy" leftover thought from the feel-good tree-hugging programs from several decades ago?

Will all of this really work at work? Here is a story of how the SANKOFA Map™ and Pattern-Aware™ programs took hold in a least likely place. If it can work here, well the workplace should be a breeze.

Years ago a social worker asked me to help her design a program for inner-city teen fathers. These were boys between the ages of 14 and 19 who already had at least one, and often two or three, children. Most of these males were without jobs and many already had petty criminal records.

I had no idea how to engage these guys; and even more, what would I have to offer to head them in a more positive direction for their futures?

Then Sandra and I decided to risk it all. There was a minimal amount of money in the program and it was to pay her salary. We had a broken-down building with a poorly-heated room to meet together.

My biggest initial concern was what in Heaven's name would these twenty-five guys have to say to this middle-aged suburban white lady?

I kept telling Sandra, who was African-American, she could at least give the young men some range of familiarity and she was the one to lead the program. I would coach her via telephone and not show up personally.

Her response was, "REALLY???!!!".

Her next comment was, "Either we do this together or it is not going to happen."

So there I was, once again, the only Caucasian in a multicolored sea of African-Americans, Hispanics, and a sprinkling of Asians. Ms. Sylvia with Ms. Sandra and twenty-five kids who smelled of beer and pot and thought this was about the stupidest thing they ever were forced to do.

Oh yes; forced they were, by court decree. Just a thought before we get back to the boys. An aside ... one director of a scientific team came to me at an off-site break years ago and said with great emotion, "Sylvia, stop using the 'F' word." Now I knew I had been absolutely appropriate and my surprised response was, "Huh?"

He retorted, "Stop asking how I *FEEL.* I have no idea how I feel; I only know what I think!"

When I went to take a break I thought, "Hmm, meet people where they are, right?"

After that I asked the same "feeling" questions, only it sounded like, "Well, what do you think?" and I got all the feeling answers fast and furious.

Now, back to the boys.

They were required to be at all six sessions and so they brought footballs to throw around, and iPods to listen to music, and comic books to read while we chattered on.

Sandra had been a teen mother who pulled herself out of some very difficult places. When she became pregnant at 15 her boyfriend, the love of her young life, deserted her and she had to face the shame and guilt dumped on her by her mother who had also had Sandra when she was sixteen.

We figured if we could get these kids to follow through and do their SANKOFA Maps™ then we had something to market to the rest of the world.

The first two sessions were one step away from worthless; and while we attempted to get the guys thinking and talking with each other, it stayed with jokes and silly target practice, throwing the footballs around whenever we so much as turned to the side.

In session three we showed them how to do their SANKOFA Map™. Suddenly there was a change in the temperature of the room.

Sandra presented her SANKOFA Map™ and was able to talk about the hurt, pain and fear she experienced and her ambivalence about giving birth to a boy rather than a girl.

It became very warm even though the heat on this cold winter day worked only sporadically. It was quiet.

A few of the pioneers in the room began to ask questions. "How can I ask my mother about getting pregnant? She'll swat me across the head."

And even more poignant were the ones who said, "I have no idea where my father is, so how do I find out about his life?"

Session four and there they were. All except two had some variation of a SANKOFA Map™ and were ready to take the leap into the past. Those who said they could not or were not willing to get information were asked to just listen and stay in the room anyway.

Each had an action plan to go back and speak to a family member, to the girl who was the mother of their child, and talk about what they had learned.

Session five was simply astounding.

The young men came in with pressed shirts and pants and the smell was of aftershave rather than alcohol.

They talked and talked and talked. And there were tears and sadness.

The essence of the tears and sadness was they did not want to repeat the patterns from the past. They did not want to ignore their children. They did not want to make fun of the girls who had opened hearts and legs for them. They did not want to talk about the mothers of their children the way they heard other fathers talk with such anger and disrespect.

By the last session almost all had jobs, and saw any job as better than hanging around at the corner bar. They did not want to pass on the legacy of avoidance and victimhood to their children. They wanted to become the role models their fathers were not able to be. They also wanted to talk with their fathers and reconnect with them in new, more appropriate ways.

They wanted to *heal the past to free the present.* And the follow-up eighteen months later showed at least 70 percent of the young men did make substantial life changes.

And the ones who made changes also began to tell their stories to friends and encourage them to "get a piece of paper and put those circles and squares on it. It will be good for you."

Chapter 32: Endless Opportunities

The world has become one great big global melting pot. We are ready to move past the little boxes of the past where we were stuck in "for and against, better or worse."

Diversity has been historically managed by statistics.

Until recently diversity has been to manage differences. It has become a policy to have so many of this or that type at work, whether we want to or not. It has been about being politically correct and avoiding class action suits and "proving" that there are no prejudices in MY Company.

Diversity Today IS
About Mindset

It is about seeing ourselves and others as UNIQUE and CONNECTED rather than merely different. What I learned working with the teen fathers is that when universal truths are touched, there is a flame of under-standing that is fanned and can become a game changer surfacing untapped intelligence and motivation regardless of the starting point of education or job title.

There is a billboard that surfaces every so often showing some inner-city kids and it says, "A mind is a terrible thing to waste." We are wasting so many good people by placing them in little boxes and not igniting the spark of seeing the uniqueness in each of us.

Organizations that hear the call of the new way of diversity management will be the winners of this century. The competencies required today are those that live through everyone in the organization starting with the CEO.

Offering employees the tools to find the way OUT (Observe, Understand, Transform) of ingrained behavior patterns from family and culture that may have worked when one was five or seven or twelve, and need to be stamped "outdated for adults," will foster collaboration.

The core competencies include education and training to foster understanding and better decision-making. This comes about when the "NOTS" that have become "KNOTS" are untied and we see each other more clearly.

Personal branding is not just marketing lingo, it is what we all need now ... to know who we are, how we arrived here, and that we have the capacity to heal the past to free the present. We all have a story to tell; and being able to decide how to say who we are in an authentic voice is key to reaching the universal wisdom that truly resides in each of us.

Self-knowledge is at the root of all great storytelling and all great positive leadership. Once you have begun to understand your own humanity and crack the code on how systems work, and that we really are all connected through time and space, then humbleness and an ability to transcend the petty moments of the day occur.

We just need to learn how to access our own deep wisdom and discuss the action steps for effective communication.

Chapter 33: Looking Toward the Future

What happens when dynamic leaders transform diversity to spark new ways of working together?

Obviously my answer is that good things begin to happen at work and in the community. And yes, that is the truth. When people feel safe, when they feel appreciated, when they are heard, that is when creativity starts to bubble up and we go into what scientists call the "flow" state.

When leaders become pattern aware, they take those 13 most annoying patterns from childhood and flip them over. And here are the 13 most vital traits that come from the hard work of leadership transformation.

PatternAware™ Leadership is for the "A-TEAM" and includes authenticity, accountability, accuracy, action, and achievement.

Take another look and see where you still have work to do. (Clue: You ALWAYS still have work to do.)

• **Creative Collaborators** are not so focused on individual accomplishments. The "me, me, me" chant changes to "we, we, we" and they know the success of the team, of the company, trumps fame and fortune. The good news is that fame and fortune often comes more long term with leaders who support everyone rather than yearning for all the credit. (old pattern: super-achiever)

• **Community Builders** do not have to yell and scream about injustice. They take a magnifying glass to identify what is needed in the community and begin to look at the unique aspects of what each individual brings to the table. They are able to fan the flame and create a groundswell of support with people who want to help change happen rather than just complain. (old pattern: rebel)

• **Realizers** have sleeves rolled up, and no matter how much they used to be afraid of being criticized they move ahead at warp speed. They have a "can do" spirit that is infectious and are always painting a picture of possibilities. They know how to feel the fear, do it anyway, and help others stay with a project regardless of how daunting. There is a sense of "if I can do it so can you" that puts others at ease. (old pattern: procrastinator)

• **Humorists** can always find something to laugh about out loud. They are able to laugh at themselves and use their foibles as great examples of "nobody is perfect" and they do this with good grace. Better yet, they have mastered the timing of putting a fun spin on a situation at exactly the moment when stress is ready to derail the team, and their non-offensive humor helps build camaraderie. (old pattern: clown)

• **Visionary** leaders are always looking far into the future, gazing at the stars for inspiration. Rather than point fingers at those who have slipped and made mistakes, they are the ultimate "lemons into margaritas" folks. This leadership trait underscores being kind yet strong, and in this way helps entire teams, entire companies develop a shared vision and a way to get through the inevitable chasm of chaos that is the conflict time waster. (old pattern: persecutor)

• **Explorers** are always at the front of the line saying "we are all in it together" and encouraging new ideas and heading into new territory. They will stay close to the front lines, and yet will move over and give others an opportunity to lead also. They always ask for at least three solutions to a problem and will help teams find the best solutions and cannot abide whining and "poor us" communications. (old pattern: victim)

• **Mentors** listen and listen and listen. They know that with encouragement most people can solve their own problems faster and smarter with someone encouraging on the sideline. They will, however, offer advice in small doses when necessary. The good news is this leadership trait is about the three bears and Goldilocks: not too much, not too little, just right and just at the right time (old pattern: rescuer)

• **Storytellers** have read this book over and over. They use stories to teach about life and leadership. They have traded in the PowerPoint for fact-based stories riddled with emotions so the learning will go deep and be implemented. This trait is vital for human connection and can be used in all forms of technology, even short and simple stories that are usually "sweet tweets." (old pattern: drama queen/king)

• **Integrators** can look at each individual's unique ability to contribute and help them find their ideal spot on a team. They are clear that while work needs to be divided fairly it is not ever one size fits all. They have the ability to help people work together without the blaming and judging that goes on when situations are not seen as equal. By the time the project is done everyone is equally proud, equally tired, and equally rewarded. (old pattern: martyr)

• **Truth Tellers** set the tone in the organization. They have learned that telling the truth is not spilling your guts. They find the perfect balance by saying "yes" to being honest and "no" to being mean-spirited. While you can expect to know where you stand with a truth teller, you can walk away with your head held high and make the changes that are being requested. Truth tellers tell the truth with dignity and will admit quickly if they messed up. (old pattern: pleaser)

• **Initiators** do not look away nor sit on the sidelines. They will stay in the middle of the fire of conflict and be a catalyst for resolution. They are time-sensitive and know that by avoiding issues that will fester they will take twice as long to resolve. By allowing the dissent of problems to stay in the room they are seen as a fair witness and there is a sense of comfort that the right decisions will come about by "staying with the pain." (old pattern: avoider)

• **Trust Builders** will not play "let's pretend." If there are issues that may mean lay-offs or major organizational change these leaders are right there saying, "We will face what is happening right here and right now." They listen to their colleagues and encourage others to tell the truth up front rather than be politically correct to save face. These leaders are willing to speak the facts without causing fear of "what if" to explode and stall progress. (old pattern: denier)

• **Peace Makers** will not side with one person or one group against another. They monitor the gossip barometer to make sure it does not get out of hand. They know there will always be some gossip yet encourage individuals to be forthright and speak directly to the source of the discomfort. These leaders are adamant that what is unique will stand in front of that which is different. (old pattern: splitter)

Chapter 34: Conclusion and New Beginnings

What does matter to all of us? To be heard and appreciated, to be acknowledged and given the space to create and care.

The world of work is one of the most amazing places for us to all grow. After all, most of us go there anyway. It does not matter if it is a Fortune 100 company, a garage start-up, a family business.

We are there not only to make money or become famous. We are there to go on a hero's journey, to learn about the parts of ourselves we have shut away in a sack in the basements of our mind.

Diversity and inclusion belong to all of us. As I said in my story, I am passionate about helping leaders deepen their authenticity so they are at the forefront of the changes this world needs to sustain itself. We cannot go on much longer fighting with those we see as different.

I do believe I have found a "cure" for different. My contribution is to help those in leadership positions create work cultures where personal storytelling, the SAN-KOFA Map™, and PatternAware™ methods can be used to see and hear each other more effectively. My hope is that this book will give you pause to look at all the individuals you work with as UNIQUE and even better consider the universal connections that can make us stronger and more productive in our work relationships, to hear each other more openly and accept each other more willingly.

I invite you to join me on this journey into the magical UNIQUE world of everyone being useful, creative and connected.

Epilogue

You know the saying "When the student is ready the teacher appears"? That is exactly what happened as I was completing this UNIQUE book. The teacher showed up in the form of films, articles, and information on the Internet. I want to pass all of this on to you that I hope will spark interest in continued learning.

A conversation with my daughter Julie sent me back to Google after we talked. "Mom, why does all this 'stuff' about patterns really matter anyway? It sometimes seems impossible to break free from repeating the past." This was said in response to a discussion we were having about her elementary school-age children who are exactly the same age difference of two-and-a-half years that she is with her sister. While Julie has a daughter and a son, patterns of sibling behavior are still there even though many of the ways of parenting have changed. We went on to talk about sibling behaviors going back as far as we could to great-grandparents.

By the time we finished we were in agreement that destiny is amazingly complex, and the more we can bring the invisible to the visible realm the better armed we are to make positive changes and "stand on the shoulders of the past" rather than repeat it.

With the Internet as a resource it is now so much easier to find out about the past. HOWEVER … and this is the warning on the bottle: it is not just about facts, it is about how the facts become emotional inventory for you to look at and then decide what you want to keep and what needs to be changed.

Here are some really good internet resources for you. www.ancestry.com does a great job. We even had someone in our Total Leadership Connections™ program find her half-sister through this site. They met and are now friends. The gal in our program said it was like finding the last few pieces to put her whole puzzle together.

Another site that is becoming very popular is www.23andme.com where you can trace your lineage back 10,000 years and discover aspects of your history from over 750 maternal lineages and 500 paternal lineages. It is another way to build your family tree. It is done with saliva testing and can be a real "aha" experience. We just ordered the kit and I certainly am curious about what I will find.

There are more and more articles about our connections with the past. Recently in the *New York Times Sunday Review* (Sunday; February 23, 2014) there was an article "Your Ancestors, Your Fate," that discusses research about how your family name indicates your level of possible success. The research shows that we stay closer to our family heritage than we like to think and that genes predict life chances more than culture or money do.

While the notion of genetic transmission of "social competence" (a mysterious mix of drive and ability) may be unsettling, it is the push to do SANKOFA Mapping™ and be in charge of consciously deciding about these patterns from the past and how to make personal, positive change happen.

You will hear more and more about genetic transmission now that we have sophisticated scientific technology available. New research from Emory University School of Medicine in Atlanta has shown that it is possible for some information to be inherited biologically through chemical changes that occur in the DNA. The research indicates that the experiences of a parent, even before conceiving offspring, markedly influence both structure and function in the nervous system of subsequent generations.

See more at:
http://www.spiritscienceandmetaphysics.com
And another bit of information came from Australia showing that how your toes are positioned will tell you about your long-ago roots. Shows that I go back to Greece and my husband Herb's lineage goes to Egypt; who knew?!!

To see what your toes have to tell you, go to http://www.news.com.au/lifestyle/relationships.

Here are a few really good films that show how patterns work within us.

In *Chocolat,* an artfully-done film, you get a clear understanding of how two very different people, the Mayor of the town who is steeped in religion and the stranger who comes into the town to open a chocolate shop, are seemingly at opposite ends of the pendulum with their patterns and yet, underneath, are both avoiders.

Sabrina shows the sibling relationship with an older, super-achiever brother in a family business who has to manage work as well as his procrastinator younger brother.

The Cider House Rules shows the power of returning to the source in this rendition of John Irving's novel. The last scenes pull the patterns together.

The Godfather is a classic about family patterns and how hard it is to move beyond them. I wonder what choices Michael Corleone would have made if he had the opportunity to do his SANKOFA Map™.

On Golden Pond shows a father-daughter relationship while underlining the pattern of avoidance. Jane Fonda has written about her experience in this film and how difficult it was to "act" in her role with her famous father Henry.

The Missing Picture is a documentary by Rithy Panh who uses clay figures to re-enact his childhood memories of the Cambodian genocide. Going back through this traumatic time he talks about the power of memory to heal. Mr. Panh goes beyond the atrocities of the millions who died and states that "behind each life lost there was a UNIQUE human being."

Living in Conflict is an award-winning documentary by Mikayla Lev about the Israeli-Palestinian conflict from the eyes of artists and poets who can see beyond the differences.

Kinky Boots is both a film and an award-winning musical on Broadway. It is very "today" about how to celebrate the "Unique" qualities of gender differences that can no longer be kept in the background. The creativity that comes from finding new ways to relate shines through in this show.

Also, here are some books you can learn a lot from.

Thinking Fast and Slow, by Daniel Kahneman. How we think either fast and emotional or slower and logical. This is critical to understanding the effect of cognitive biases.

Quiet: The Power of Introverts in a World That Can't Stop Talking, by Susan Cain. About how to manage the diversity of introverts and extroverts at work.

Some of My Best Friends are Black: The Strange Story of Integration in America, by Tanner Colby. Uses story to uncover the deep emotions surrounding race.

The Medici Effect: What Elephants and Epidemics Can Teach Us About Innovation, by Frans Johansson. Looks at the intersection where concepts from diverse cultures and industries collide to spark new ideas.

The Inclusion Dividend: Why Investing in Diversity and Inclusion Pays Off, by Mark Kaplan. In today's diverse world, D and I is a core leadership competency and central to business success.

The Inclusion Breakthrough: Unleashing the Real Power of Diversity, by Frederick Miller. How creativity and good will come from a new and more powerful way of including those who are "different."

Make your own list of literature and film. Also look deeply at today's news and you will find patterns of the past reflected all around you.

Tell your story.

Tell it to "heal the past and free the present." Tell your story to help others see their life stories more clearly. Each story is vital, each of us has a light inside that needs to become a flame in the world.

Each story is UNIQUE. Each story matters.

Author's Page

Sylvia Lafair, PhD, has dedicated her career to helping individuals become their best. First as a psychologist working with families and couples and then making a left-hand turn into the world of business leadership and team development.

Her "UNIQUE" ideas have had widespread influence in corporations, family firms, and entrepreneurial startups.

The past 25 years have been spent helping executives, managers, and teams connect the dots of how personal and professional behavior cannot be separated. She has trained a staff of executive coaches and facilitators in her PatternAware™ model.

What has been eye-opening in all manner of organizations is that when stress hits the hot button we all tend to revert to patterns from childhood that were there to keep us safe. While they may have helped at five or seven or twelve, they can wreak havoc in adult relationships.

Working with companies around the world, it became clear that the universal aspects of what it means to be in relationships is not very different regardless of culture, size of company, or product. Everywhere there is the yearning for all of us to get along. Dr. Lafair's innovative work gives us the directives to make this happen.

Her book *Don't Bring It to Work* has won nine awards, and with its companion *Pattern Aware Success Guide,* has been used in graduate programs and by work teams worldwide.

Her book *GUTSY: How Women Leaders Make Change* has also won six book awards and led to her highly-successful "GUTSY Women Weekend Retreats."

This newest book *UNIQUE: How Story Sparks Diversity, Inclusion and Engagement,* is based on the powerful model of storytelling called SANKOFA Mapping™.

Dr. Lafair's abilities to blend story with fact and humor make her a sought-after speaker, workshop facilitator, and executive coach.

Her Total Leadership Connections™ program, now in its fourteenth year, has been named one of the top leadership development programs for 2014 by Leadership Excellence/H.R.com, making this the third year in a row.

Dr. Lafair has been featured in the *Wall Street Journal, Forbes* and *Time* as well as on the *Today Show* with Kathie Lee and Hoda.

For further information or to book Dr. Lafair for a consultation or speaking engagement, please call her office in Pennsylvania at 570-636-3858, or e-mail her directly at sylvia@ceoptions.com.

Printed in Great Britain
by Amazon.co.uk, Ltd.,
Marston Gate.